No Man's Lands:

eight extraordinary women
in Balkan history

No Man's Lands:

eight extraordinary women in Balkan history

Elizabeth Gowing
& Robert Wilton

No Man's Lands:

eight extraordinary women in Balkan history

By Elizabeth Gowing and Robert Wilton

First published in 2022 by Elbow Publishing

Chapters 6 and 7 draw on material previously published by the
same author in the *London Magazine* and *Symbol*.

A catalogue record for this book is available from the British
Library

ISBN: 978-1-9163661-1-4

Cover design: Su Jones and Paddy McEntaggart
Cover photograph used with kind permission of the Museum of
the City of Belgrade
Design and typesetting: Sally Ellis-Rudd

for Diella and Adena
and for all the girls who are growing up in the Balkans
writing new chapters

Contents

Introduction

In a frontier region notorious for division and war, pioneering women have been overshadowed by warrior men, women's voices have been drowned out by demagogues and shell-fire, and the distinctive realities and challenges of women have been buried in the rubble of other conflicts.

The effort to challenge this is still the business of a new generation of battle-hardened activists – some of whose voices are heard in these pages – and of well-meant if synthetic international projects. Although the region is now seeing impressive women rising to the top of almost every profession, including some female presidents and prime ministers, they are too often seen as curiosities or tokens regardless of ability, and too often analysed and criticised for their conformity to traditional norms of femininity (looks, decorum) and in derogatory sexist terms. And although wider social changes are starting to re-balance the expectations within relationships, the majority of those modern professional women will still be expected to resume the most traditional women's roles as soon as they get home. Midnight strikes early every day for the Balkan Cinderella.

In countries whose security or identity still feels threatened, children are brought up with a strong, simple – even mythic – patriotism, built around male heroes. Most countries call on one or more mediaeval warrior titans, a generation of late nineteenth-century or early twentieth-century statesmen and male cultural pioneers, and often some late twentieth-century liberators. The street names and statues of Balkan cities represent a very skewed world-view. The characterisation of the few heroines with profile – like Shote Galica, in chapter six – is nuanced to reinforce gender norms: they were still somehow feminine despite, or they were forced to be regrettably unfeminine because of, their circumstances.

This is not a distinctly Balkan phenomenon, and no other country or culture is yet in a position to preach about equality. But some aspects of Balkan history – social conservatism, the distractions of horrific wars and other battles of identity – have exacerbated the problem.

This collection of essays is intended as a small contribution to the ongoing and essential effort more fairly to represent the position of women in Balkan history and society, and more energetically to drive some much-needed progress towards real equality. It also reflects the belief, embodied in diverse aspects of our work over the years, that the culture and history of the Balkans deserve to be more widely known, and that our world is healthier when we engage with other cultures instead of effacing or excluding them.

We have engaged with this region originally as enthralled visitors, and now as contented citizens. Our experiences have been defined by our original status as guests – by the hospitality and humanity and hope of the people who have welcomed us. But in the best part of twenty years working and living in the region we have also seen the failings, the weaknesses and the scars. Ours has been a fortunate, but not an unreal Balkans. As development, education and governance professionals we have worked in the offices of the most senior political leaders, and on the doorsteps of the most disadvantaged and marginalised of Europe's citizens. As activists we have worked and advocated to promote universal themes of equality, education, environment and heritage, and to enable the excluded to be heard. As writers, we have tried in a variety of ways and works not to criticise, but humbly and honestly to explore, the region that has become our home.

To pick out the stories of eight individual women is of course highly whimsical and wholly undemocratic. But we are not professional scholars of gender or society, and we cannot try to depict a generalised or scientific truth. We are both story-tellers and, by exploring the individual lives of eight diverse and impressive women, we hope to give fresh focus to at least a few of the endless lives that deserve it, and we hope through them to illuminate their societies and the female experience in the Balkans.

We do think these women were all remarkable: illuminatingly typical yet interestingly unusual. Seven were natives of the seven countries that make up today's loosely defined western Balkans: Albania, Bosnia-Herzegovina, Croatia, Kosovo, Montenegro, North Macedonia and Serbia. Each in their way was out of the ordinary; yet each has something to tell us about ordinariness for women then and now. The eighth is included to represent a related phenomenon: many generations of foreign men have come to the Balkans, as soldiers and diplomats and spies and theorists, and their work has not on the whole been welcomed or remembered with any great fondness; it has been women who have come, as travellers and humanitarians and ethnographers, and been accepted and celebrated. It is women who immersed themselves more fully, and have endured more powerfully in the popular memory.

We don't think any of our eight met each other. But then, this is not a story about a network or a movement. We are happy to think of them being brought together for the first time here – a selection of voices, just a few among a multitude who deserve to be heard.

Elizabeth Gowing & Robert Wilton
Prishtina, 2022

Map of places mentioned in the text

Timeline

1830	1840	1850	1860	1870	1880	1890	1900	1910

Staka Skenderova
1831-1891

Marija Jurić Zagorka
1873-1957

Xenia Petrović-Njegoš
1881-1960

Maga Magazinović
1882-1968

Margaret Hasluck
1885-1948

Shote Galica
1895-1927

1930	1940	1950	1960	1970	1980	1990	2000	2010

Musine Kokalari
1917-1983

Esma Redžepova
1943-2016

Pronunciation Guide

This book explores lands dominated by two completely different linguistic traditions, albeit both Indo-European. Macedonian (and Slovenian), and the language spoken in different forms in what are now Bosnia-Herzegovina, Croatia, Serbia, and Montenegro (and by a significant number of Slavs elsewhere in the western Balkans), sit on the Slavic branch of the Indo-European tree. Albanian, meanwhile, sits on its own branch (a squirrel, perhaps, guarding rare and tasty linguistic nuts such as the admirative verb form).

The following guide is neither exhaustive nor very nuanced; for ease of reference in this context, instead of separating by language it merely offers a hint about less familiar sounds as they arise. Both language families are much more regular than English, and many letters are pronounced as they often are in English; 'f' is always the sound at the beginning of 'feminist'.

C	like the 'ts' in *diplomats*
Č	a hard 'ch', as in *teacher*
Ç	a hard 'ch', as in *teacher*
Ć	a slightly (sometimes imperceptibly) softer 'ch'
Dh	like the 'th' in *them*
Dj	(in the Slav languages) like the 'j' in *journalist*
Dž	like the 'j' in *journalist*
Ë	like the 'er' in *teacher*
Gj	like the 'j' in *journalist*
J	like the 'y' in *years*
L	like the 'l y' in *several years*
Ll	like the 'l' in *literature*
Q	a slightly (sometimes imperceptibly) softer 'ch'
Rr	a rolled 'r'
Š	like the 'sh' in *shot*
X	like the 'ds' in *words*
Xh	like the 'j' in *journalist*
Y	like the 'u' in the French *tu*
Ž	as in the middle of *pleasure*
Zh	as in the middle of *pleasure*

Chapter 1

Passing as a man: Staka Skenderova and a Sarajevo education

Stand at the Žuta Tabija just before sunset and you have a rose-tinted view of the city of Sarajevo rolled out like a patterned prayer mat before you.

Boom! It's from this bastion that during the holy month of Ramadan a cannon is fired each night to mark the end of the daylight fast. It's a signal that the time has come first for prayer and then for a reverent sip of cool water after the day's parching, and the heady sugar rush of the traditional nibbled date before the full iftar meal begins.

From this vantage point you can look down at the city's landmarks: its history as the 'Jerusalem of the West' with the Ashkenazi synagogue, the cathedral, and Gazi Huzrev-Beg's mosque and library.

You can look at the Latin Bridge where the cack-handed shot was fired that almost, but didn't quite, miss Archduke Franz Ferdinand, whose blood mingled with that of twenty million others by the time the First World War had run its course.

And while you're thinking of war you can squint at the nineteenth-century City Hall, admiring its Moorish arches and garish stripes, and think of all the books that have been stored there – 1.5 million volumes and over 155,000 rare books and manuscripts at the height of the collection. You can think of all that this represents – the endless hours of labour, the mingling thoughts of great brains, the dreams that words can kindle in the minds of readers. While you're squinting, you can imagine you're a soldier posted on this Sarajevan hillside on 25 August 1992, looking through a sight and deciding to shell the library: shell it thoroughly enough that it will burn to the ground and its collection will be destroyed.

These hills offer a panorama of the city. They offer coolth and recreation for its stifled inhabitants during the summer. They offered a bobsleigh route and ski slopes for the 1984 Olympics, while Torvill and Dean sparkled on the flat. And they offer a deadly advantage for any army wanting to take the city under siege, as the Serbs did for 1,425 days during the Bosnian War. Some 14,000 people died, most picked off by snipers at vantage points like this who were targeting civilians, many of them children, walking across market-places, queueing for food, playing in the street.

From here the individuals would have been clear to see. We can zoom in on them now, the little people ant-like in streets below, with white faces which bloom into the features of an old man, a teenager, families, groups of friends, when shot with a good camera lens.

White, too, are the graveyards which stud the outskirts of the city. And here, too, the faceless impression of human frailty takes a more meaningful shape when you zoom in on the details of dates and places. This is a child; here is someone far from home; a husband and wife dying in the same week (victims of the same accident or pandemic or grief?). Some have photographs. I am looking carefully now because the graveyard is the purpose of this trip. I have come to Sarajevo not for a generalised fix of memento mori; I am looking for someone in particular. Where is Staka Skenderova?

∼

Staka Skenderova's death, on 26th May 1891, tends to be told with an amplified pity. The 60-year-old retired teacher was walking in Sarajevo's Ilidža suburb, popular for excursions, when she was knocked down by a horse-and-carriage. She was tended by a friend, but could not long survive her injuries.

The manner of her death emphasises frailty, vulnerability: the pedestrian falling to the vehicle; the person too deaf to hear or too slow to avoid the threat; the victim dependent on the care of others. In one account she was escorting two poor orphan children who had been on a day out: the pity is multiplied, and the children's survival adds a hint of self-sacrifice by the one who did not. Her death is told as some kind of natural extension of her circumstances in the later part of her life: her school had been forced to close; she was living in poverty.

Is this final bathos meant to be a painful irony contrasting with her earlier success and achievement? Is it meant merely to illustrate the plight that affected many women? Skenderova is not the only woman in this book whose prominence and activism were seen as unnatural as well as unusual, and were followed by later lives of reported difficulty and solitude and untimely death. Is there the faintest suggestion that women who transgress in that way should not be surprised to find themselves poor and lonely and falling under runaway horses?

She was born in what was still Ottoman Sarajevo, in 1831 (some sources say 1828 or 1830), the daughter of Serb immigrants. Multi-cultural Bosnia, and apocryphally the diverse clientele of her brother's tailoring business, exposed her apparently hungry mind to different languages and sectors of society, and she grew up unusually literate and cultured. In 1858 she opened Sarajevo's first school for girls. This milestone achievement was made more unprecedented by her willingness to admit pupils from the city's different ethnic and religious groups, to subsidise poorer pupils, and to show no discrimination in her desperate search for funding.

Her energy to communicate and educate was grounded in an identity of place. She published her *Annals of Bosnia 1825-1856* in 1859 – just a year after opening her school. It was also grounded in an identity of status: she became known as a critic of exploitative merchants and a legal advocate for the poor. *The Biographical Dictionary of Women's Movements and Feminisms* describes her as 'A trailblazer... a pioneer in education... the country's first social worker, as well as its first published woman author' and as the first in a long line of culturally and socially influential women.

Staka Skenderova's life was defined by her willingness to cross boundaries political as well as social. Her fund-raising – and surely some deeper drive – took her to Belgrade, Constantinople and Jerusalem. Hers was a distinctively Sarajevan cosmopolitanism, though it's rare to find it encompassed within one Bosnian rather than a diverse collection of them. But in the end her realities were more constrained than her vision: shortage of funds; the Austro-Hungarian occupation of Bosnia-Herzegovina; a fire. The school closed and Skenderova had to rely on the charity of others to live: a dependency of survival, rather than of the expansive energy of her pioneering days. The summaries of her life are silent on its last dozen years.

∾

Skenderova's life and achievements were defined by her femininity, and they were equally defined by her need to navigate, negotiate, extend and transcend the perceptions of her femininity. Hers is a story not only of womanliness defiant, but also of 'womanliness' defied. As well as the restraints imposed on her identity, she has had to struggle against the restraints of the representation of her identity.

Almost all of the accounts of Skenderova's life emphasise the fact that she was a woman. The point of almost all of them, indeed, is the fact that she was a woman – the first published woman author, and so on. Her achievements are presented as significant because of it; she achieved 'despite' it. Having stressed her femininity, the accounts then begin to describe how she did not behave in a manner consistent with her femininity. She was unusual because she was a woman, and she was unusual as a woman.

She 'wore black, men's clothes and a headscarf'. 'She smoked tobacco, went out to cafes and never married.'

'From a young age, her father dressed her in men's clothing, as Christians and Muslims living in Bosnia often did with their young daughters. She continued this habit throughout her life.' Some accounts remember to mention that these details were in part tactics to help her engage effectively in the circles she needed to, running a public enterprise, raising money. 'Men's suits released [her] from being confined in the household environment, gave [her] easy access to the circle of men', suggests the account of her by the Medica Zenica activist organisation. The man's costume 'was clearly one of the ways to achieve freedom of movement and live differently to what was ordained'. Her apparently masculine habits - the cafes, the drinking, the smoking – 'were only a small element of the equality [she] fought for, while the most important was [her] engagement in society'. Both her costume and the over-wrought representation of her costume have echoes of Anne Lister, the lesbian nineteenth-century English landowner. 'I have entered upon my plan to always wear black,' Lister declared, and it is now interpreted as emphasising a masculine identity or grief at a relationship suppressed. Most accounts present Skenderova's habits to modern readers as examples of her inherent unconventionality – even defiance.

Sometimes she is described as having become a nun during her visit to Jerusalem. In others she just dressed like a nun. It turns out that the religious significance of taking the vow is less distinctive than the social significance of behaving as if she had done so. She was 'called a nun because she looked like that in behavior and dress - she wore a man's suit'. Three different re-presentations of identity collide in the sentence: to behave in a certain way was nunnish; to dress in a certain way was nunnish; and, paradoxically, wearing a man's suit was nunnish. The first – behaving with restraint and deference – is an amplification of what is supposed to be feminine. ('She was humble and withdrawn, and very pious', says another writer, with a hint that this was a welcome counter-balance to her otherwise unnatural behaviour, and even a welcome improvement on some women's flightiness and boldness.) The second – dressing soberly – is an adaptation or even a suppression. The third is renunciation. For one writer, Skenderova's clothing was a symbol of having renounced marriage. For another, achieving her aims obliged Skenderova not only to put on men's clothes but also to 'renounce her maidenhood'. For these writers, Skenderova is undoubtedly a heroine (albeit dressed as a hero); her story includes a strong sense of something sacrificed, and by extension an acknowledgement that there had been positive or desirable aspects of the prescribed feminine identity which she had chosen to abandon. Instead of foregoing the pleasures of uncloistered life in order to achieve a closer communion with God, Sister Staka forewent the pleasures of the cloister in order to smoke and drink and achieve a closer communion with potential sponsors. This meant, regardless, giving up the ideas of motherhood and wifehood – for better or for worse. Everyone emphasises her liberated achievement, but they also emphasise that lonely pathetic death.

We know how this was seen – at least, all of the modern accounts are clear about how it would have been seen – at the time. But how is Staka Skenderova's chosen identity really seen today? Is there still a lurking sense of a choice unfortunate and undesirable, as well as unnatural and unusual?

'Representations of anyone's femininity or masculinity should not be a topic of discussion, at least today,' says Masha Durkalić from Sarajevo; she and her creator-activist colleagues, Hatidža Gušić and Amila Hrustić Batovanja, led the #ŽeneBiH project to research and publicise the lives of significant women in the history of Bosnia-Herzegovina (BiH). 'However, at her time, this was most probably considered as scandalous. The historical accounts that say that Staka wore male clothes, smoked, and went to cafes, have a different significance. They show the way that women were fighting to occupy the space they rightly deserved, by employing tactics which would involve them in the business of men. Staka was a pioneer in this sense, when even today society is still scandalised if women don't conform to the standard gender roles or ideas of how women should look and act.'

Skenderova's pioneering role as an educator had an extra dimension: she was a woman teacher of young women; hers was Sarajevo's first school for girls. While attempts to analyse her own status risk becoming bogged down in debates about representation, her impact on those young lives and on the concept of the education of women is clearer.

Skenderova is typically described as, or assumed to have been, a hungry reader – like every other woman of significance you've ever heard of from before about 1950. It's telling that some further aspect of unusualness is sought to explain the phenomenon of 'women who did things', and it's telling that this was women's only chance at education before women like her began to offer a formal path. But a path to what? Skenderova's pupils were taught reading, writing and arithmetic – the traditional tools for stronger communication and functionality in society – and also handcrafts. Craft-work might be another channel of self-actualisation; it might be the basis for economic development and autonomy; it might also be what women were expected to be good at in the traditional model of society. According to one author, Skenderova's graduates 'were considered to be very eligible brides, and they married well'. This is not to diminish in any way the impact of Staka Skenderova or the characters and abilities of her pupils, but it's a reminder of the framework in which they were required to function. The sentence comes off as more complimentary about the discerning husbands of Sarajevo, and at best back-handed about their brides' education.

Skenderova's distinction and impact is reinforced by a strong element of intersectionality. In her school, the fees of rich parents subsidised the education of poor children. In some descriptions this assumes a broader activism: 'Staka advocated social equality, and was a fierce critic of the cadre of wealthy Serbian merchants, whom she openly accused of exploiting their poorer compatriots', declares #ŽeneBiH. This in turn echoes the social and indeed patriotic advocacy running through her book, *The Annals of Bosnia*. Skenderova reputedly petitioned for and represented poorer (Turkish-speaking) citizens in court, visited and helped prisoners, and campaigned for civic improvements.

The emphasis of this further aspect of her activism also hints at a further aspect of stereotyping. The depiction of the exhaustive range of her charitability tends to render her not merely kindly but saintly. Male pioneers and activists may be presented as warriors, but for their female equivalents a more seemly image is sought. (Joan of Arc is the epitome of female warriorhood, but also of male outrage at this breach of the proper order. One of the charges against her during her trial was the wearing of male clothing in combat – when she found it a little more practical – and in confinement – when she found it hampered her guards' attempts to rape her.) There can be no doubt of Skenderova's resilience and courage and defiance. But there's a risk that – lest these virtues seem inappropriate – they are presented as no more than characteristics taken on, with her manly garb, in order to realise her inherent womanly goodliness. It's another way in which representing her as a nun not only explains and validates her activism, but also confines it.

The story of Staka Skenderova incorporates a patriotic element: writing the *Annals* was both an indigenous act of nation-defining and an assertion of nation-centric historical truths. For scholar Celia Hawkesworth, the chronicle is focused on the resilience of the Bosnian instinct to autonomy. 'In numerous historical analyses,' writes another commentator, 'we will find data that the education of female children in Bosnia and Herzegovina began after Austro-Hungary occupied these areas. This is not true, because Staka Skenderova opened the first school for girls'. Bosnia needed imposed foreign values no more than it needed imposed foreign identity.

Yet much of her story is defined by – celebrates, indeed – the ways in which she engaged with the foreign. And as I navigate Sarajevo today – rekindling an old friendship to co-ordinate my visit; following threads of diplomatic and activist acquaintanceship to learn some new perspectives – the complexity of her network resonates. The realities of empire made it necessary for Skenderova to engage with the Ottoman hierarchy, locally and in Constantinople. It was natural that she found support in Belgrade for the education of Bosnia's Serbian children. That Slav affinity and her own determination led her to tap Russian support too. The support of Russia's consul in Bosnia, Alexander Hilferding (or Gilferding or Guilferding), is usually presented as critical to her success. He is said to have encouraged her to write the *Annals*, and published and translated the work. He arranged financial backing for the new school. According to one account, a change in consul saw a drop in support.

This is consistent with a wider pattern in Balkan national culture. The obligatory dictionaries and orthographies and folk song collections and verse epics, and of course annals, were in themselves strong statements of creative autonomy and cultural distinctiveness. The patriots who produced them are rightly celebrated. And yet this activity was frequently inspired, prompted, facilitated or supported by intermediaries representing or bridging to some wider cultural context. The legendary Vuk Karadžić, godfather of Serbian national and folk literature, was enabled by a supportive official in Vienna. Montenegro's cultural flourishing benefited, like Skenderova, from Russian support. The ideals and culture of Albanian nationalism flourished in Bucharest, Cairo, Constantinople, Italy and the United States. None of this is surprising, and nor does it diminish the indigenous achievements. The intermediaries represented greater freedom of action, or sympathetic funding, or a more literate audience. In some cases they represented political calculation, too: it was congenial to Russian interests in the Balkans to have a flourishing Slavic Bosnian identity.

In its cosmopolitan dimensions, Skenderova's story overlaps with that of another extraordinary woman: the British educator, humanitarian, activist and writer Paulina Irby. Irby travelled widely in south-eastern Europe and wrote serious analyses of the social conditions she found, was once arrested as a spy, distributed food to refugees during the Bosnian revolt, and promoted, raised funds for and organised schools in Bosnia. She spent much of her later life in Sarajevo, and was long remembered – and is still commemorated in Sarajevo and Belgrade – as 'Miss Irby'. When Staka Skenderova's school was forced to close, Irby looked after not only her but also her work, opening another school for girls. With the status of beneficent Great Power guest rather than local curiosity, and the social and charitable resources of London behind her, Irby was able to institutionalise Skenderova's innovation.

There is, just occasionally in the histories, a sense of or a sensitivity about a possible 'white saviour' phenomenon: the more affluent, more powerful, more cosmopolitan foreigner enabling the local success, and showing how it should be done. This seems unfair on Skenderova – her achievement as well as her ability – and indeed on Miss Irby and the people of Sarajevo. The respective experiences of the two women imply a strong mutual respect and mutual support. Indeed, one account describes an incident in which Miss Irby's school was threatened with a church- and municipality-led boycott of its 'Lutheran' tendencies, but was saved by Skenderova's persuasive public intervention. Irby's enterprise, nonetheless, was more resilient to the forces of economics and politics than Skenderova's, with its perpetual financial fragility and the greater vulnerability of its founder to local expectations. For Masha Durkalić, 'the name of Miss Irby, who actually supported Staka with education for girls, but who came after Staka, is much more well-known… Staka, like many other women from BiH history, has been rendered invisible'. Is this merely politeness to a generous foreigner, or an enduring indifference to the struggles of a pioneering indigenous woman?

For Skenderova, as for others like her, there was a necessary navigation of the empires and the Europe in which they found themselves: a credit to their enterprise and skill, and no detriment to their creativity and independence of spirit. To different degrees, twenty-first century Sarajevo and Prishtina and other Balkan capitals remain colonial societies: international diplomats have more influence over national leaders than do their own citizens; international NGOs have greater resources and clout, while local NGOs depend on European Union or foreign Embassy funding; activists have much greater chance of getting a headline in their own media if they can attract an Ambassador onto their platform. Outside the Balkans, Balkan literature is known only in translation. In the nineteenth century, as in the twenty-first, the most adept Bosnian campaigner is a most adept internationalist.

∼

No country in the world has achieved gender equality, and Bosnia and Herzegovina is part of that', says Durkalić. 'The struggles that have been taking place have undoubtedly affected the state of gender equality, and they continue to do so. We have a very small share of women's participation in public and political life, and therein lies the biggest issue – women are not being invited to take their earned part in public life, because of the still predominant opinion that the public sphere is for men, and the private sphere is for women. This is a concept that needs to be overturned.' According to UN Women, 'women in Bosnia and Herzegovina have one of the region's lowest economic activity rates, and live a precarious reality: disproportionately subject to violence, they have limited access to employment and face deep-rooted patriarchal stereotypes that marginalise them and exclude them from political and decision-making processes.'

Bosnia has spent the last thirty years preoccupied with whether and how it can be a country, and issues that cut across national and ethnic lines have to an extent been pushed aside. It is another echo of Skenderova's era and her campaigns, fighting for oxygen between the ambitions of Ottomans, Austrians, Russians and others.

Sarajevo remains an icon of wounded European cosmopolitanism, everything contained and represented by the City Hall visible from the hill. The city was the epitome of the Yugoslav dream of sustainable multi-ethnic diversity and, looking down from the hill, the cockpit of its bloody collapse. When agitated or threatened, ethnic identity became the touchstone of insecurity and viciousness. But though the city is now notorious for that desecration of an ideal, what's impressive is how few years over the past half dozen centuries have been marked by inter-communal conflict. While the tides of empires, east and west, ebbed back and forth, the diverse peoples who had drifted to Sarajevo were left to work out a remarkable co-existence. Hence the 'Jerusalem of the West' tag; historian Noel Malcolm points out that it's one of the very few European cities to have a mosque, a synagogue, an Orthodox church and a Catholic church in close proximity. It was Skenderova's relative good fortune to live in a period when Bosnia was defined more by its relationship to external and themselves relatively diverse powers. The communities were distinct in her Sarajevo, but she was able to gather pupils and money from all directions: to suggest for a time that education was an absolute good, that not only did girls deserve it but also they deserved it regardless of identity.

The international powers that squabbled over Sarajevo and then contrived a war from it at the beginning of the twentieth century watched on at the end of the century as communities in and around the city were deprived not only of education but home, freedom and life because of their identity. Now the international community has determined that multi-ethnicity must remain possible: partly in the noble assertion that common humanity should unite more than individual identity divides, partly because of the uncomfortable precedent that the failure of multi-ethnicity would set for too many states whose borders are accidents of history and whose populations have come with the tides.

But now the imperative for different ethnic communities to co-exist is implemented through an obsessive definition by ethnicity: quotas are more important than quality throughout modern Sarajevan and Bosnian public life. A century and a half after Skenderova taught Catholic, Muslim and Jewish girls together, Bosnia has ministries of education in its Bosniak/Croat and Serb halves, and in each of the former's ten ethnically-characterised cantons, and some schools are internally segregated by ethnicity. Skenderova saw the right to education as more important than ethnic identity, and educated across those boundaries; today ethnic identity is more important, and the efficiency, quality, philosophy and content of education are made subordinate and limited by it. Obliged to be ethnic first and educated second, Bosnia's young women are discriminated against regardless of ethnicity.

Staka Skenderova is here. Beside me, her grave is part of her city, within earshot of Ramadan cannon and sniper rifle. The rights and equalities she worked for remain unrealised in this landscape. But although the local and international politicians shape the maps and statute-books, just as they did in the mid-nineteenth century, between the lines Skenderova's spirit continues to define what this place is and what it can be. Optimistic foreign diplomats and local citizens continue to believe that Skenderova's Bosnia is possible, and authentic. Her descendants in activism guard her name and her cause.

Typically unusual, her gravestone is black.

Chapter 2

Woman from beyond the hills: Marija Jurić Zagorka

The statue, in the heart of old Zagreb, is stout and matronly. Its clothing seems appropriate to the pretty Habsburg houses around: dress down to the ground and high around the throat. The hair is sculpted into a bun that once passed for dignified but never young. The bosom is mighty. Of all things, the woman is carrying an umbrella, half-opened.

The statue is unlikely, almost comic. Because why bother making a statue of someone not apparently considered heroic, or beautiful, or grand, or stylish, or distinctive in any way? The look embodies tradition, conservatism, solidly respectable reserve.

One detail more strikes you: she's moving. One foot pushes forwards through the tent of a frock, and to look at her is unsettling because to your mind she won't stand still.

⤳

There's nothing radical about the person depicted in the statue. This does not look like a pioneer. And though the statue seems an affectionate homage, prominent in the Croatian capital, near the home that's now become a memorial centre in her name, there's something about it that seems to embody very accurately the kind of scorn and belittlement that Marija Jurić endured throughout her life.

(There's a bust in another town which is considerably worse: the mighty shoulders and bosom seem to have been formed of three boulders stacked together, the hair looks like a sack of washing dropped on the head, the face is a rudimentary attempt to capture an old boxer past his prime, with a couple of plasticine eyebrows added as an afterthought.)

As a woman, Marija Jurić suffered discrimination – disadvantage, marginalisation, oppression, harassment – all her life. And it was explicitly her womanliness that was the vehicle and the language of her discrimination: she was married off as a young woman against her will, curtained off as a young journalist against the disapproving eye of male visitors to the office; she was a 'crone', a 'madwoman', a 'mannish old hag'. Her editor at the journal *Obzor* in the early years of the twentieth century declared her 'a granny without name or reputation, no one and nothing, a cowgirl infected with the socialist mentality and feminist notions', curiously linking and blithely dismissing in one phrase feminists, socialists, people from the countryside – and grandmothers.

Her achievements were remarkable, especially in the context of the disadvantages. The list of her successes is almost laughably impressive, a Napoleonic cavalcade of triumph more appropriate to the simpler glories of historical fiction. And her achievements were remarkable entirely irrespective of the disadvantages. These were not achievements despite or relative to anything. They were absolutes, which any journalist or novelist or reformer of any gender would have been delighted to reach. She achieved for women, and she burst the bounds of how society defined and validated womanhood; and so perhaps it's a shame that her memorial, however affectionate, tries to fix her for posterity so conventionally.

~

The morning sun blazes into the parlour. Its glow burns on the face of a young woman, as she stands rigid against the door post. She is small, but her large eyes blaze with passion and her every muscle is taut with her strength and her anger.

'Do you defy me?' hisses her mother.

'It is my life', says the young woman; 'it is my choice.'

'It is neither. You shall marry Mr Matraja: he is a man of superior quality and good prospects. You shall be very fortunate to carry his name and his children. You cannot fight this, and you should not.'

'I can fight it, and I must! Even if it takes my whole lifetime.'

It would seem unfair to introduce a prose stylist like Marija Jurić Zagorka in conventional biographical fashion.

Writing and struggle defined much of Zagorka's life. She edited her first newspaper while still in high school, circulating the single sheet among the other students. She was onto her second by the time she was eighteen, in 1891, adopting a male version of her name: Marija (originally Mariana) Jurić became M. Jurica Zagorski – he from the Zagorje region, literally the land 'behind the hills'. In the future she would be forced, endlessly, to defend or defy her femininity; less and less would she hide it. (It's not clear whether the male *noms de plume* she occasionally used for her early polemic writing were to increase the chance of being published or the chance of being listened to.)

There immediately followed the disastrous marriage, imposed by her mother against the wishes of Marija and her father. We only have Zagorka's and posterity's side of the story, but it clearly wasn't happy. Her husband was half a generation older than her, a Hungarian railway official apparently bigoted against Croats – such as his new young wife. (That second student paper of hers had been banned after one edition because her editorial invoked a Croatian national hero tortured and executed for leading a rebellion against Hungarian oppression, so the marriage was surely on shaky foundations.) She endured three years of this and a mental breakdown, escaped, and was sent to an asylum thanks to her husband's testimony. She managed to escape that too, and the marriage, but she was held formally responsible for its failure thanks to her own mother's testimony against her. It's hard to imagine the kind of vulnerabilities fostered by these diverse assaults on her character – as daughter, as wife, as woman – and the kind of strength she must have cultivated to endure it all. She was still only twenty-two.

Independent and/or isolated, she began to publish newspaper articles. At first she was allowed only to be a proof-reader for the *Obzor* daily because the editor and others objected to the idea of a woman writing. When they were pushed – by Bishop Josip Juraj Strossmayer, internationally prominent cleric, patriotic politician, national advocate, patron of education and of folk literature

– to overcome this anxiety, Zagorka was obliged to work behind a curtain because they objected to the sight of a woman writing. Her first article was about how exclusive use of Hungarian at railway stations discriminated against the Croat majority of the population; it's surely not too fanciful to see a dig at her Hungarian railway administrator husband.

She wrote for *Obzor* for the best part of twenty years, producing political reporting, analysis and interviews. (She would note proudly that even though Britain had suffragettes, it didn't have female political journalists.) When the editor of *Obzor* was imprisoned for a few months, she took over the rôle. She went to prison herself for organising demonstrations against the Hungarian governor. After she left *Obzor* in 1917 she wrote for and/or ran various papers and magazines for another two decades. She founded new papers or magazines of her own in 1917, 1925 (*Ženski List* – 'The Woman's Paper' – was the first Croatian paper for women) and 1939. More than once it was frustration with the conservatism of the editorial line where she worked that spurred her to set up on her own. She was among those who founded the Croatian Journalists' Association and, a generation later, the Croatian Female Writers' Association.

A forty-year career as a high-profile current affairs journalist was, especially for a woman in a conservative and politically-restrained society, significant enough. In parallel she made herself a prolific novelist. Her dozens of novels were unashamedly populist, and have remained popular. They were generally historical fiction, repainting in dramatic colours different bits of Croatia's national story, with strong elements of folklore, adventure, mystery, melodrama and the occult. Her most enduring success was the seven-novel *Grička Vještica* cycle – the English is an even more euphonous *The Witch of Grič*. Supposedly the publishers liked the first so much that they announced the impending sequel without asking the author whether one was intended. Her first novel came out when she was still in her twenties; her last nearly sixty years later.

She also wrote plays, of course. It's typical of her diverse energy that two of her more surprising achievements – remember the sturdy statue; remember the umbrella – feel like little more than footnotes to everything else she was doing. The author of technicolour historical adventures – with their secret passages, witches and gypsy curses – is also recognised as a pioneer of science-fiction writing, in the 1918 novel *Crveni Ocean* ('Red Ocean'). Oh, and a pioneer of screenwriting: she was credited with the scripts for two films, in 1917 and 1920 – a time when feature-films were still in their infancy even in America and western Europe. Typically, they're seen as the two most significant Croatian films of the pre-war era. Typically, one was based on a Croatian peasants' revolt (the same one that had got her student paper banned) and the other was based on one of her own novels. With Zagorka, there is always the sense of a relentless commitment to certain themes, and to the sheer imperative to create, to speak.

She was victimised by the fascist regime in Croatia during the Second World War, and disadvantaged by a perverse reactionary element in the Communist regime that followed it. The last decade of her life, before her death in 1957, had a bleak, fugitive vulnerability to it: now in her seventies, she felt obliged to advertise for a lodger so that her apartment wasn't commandeered for families, and so that she had someone to bring her food; the two men she accepted – in return for bequeathing them her flat and her authorial rights – apparently mistreated her.

She kept writing.

∼

The slope by the Butcher's Tower has become a human ant-hill. A grey dusk hangs over the crowd that has gathered at Zvjezdišće. The frost creaks underfoot, the air stings one's face, but people stand as if frozen by the snow, and wait.

At the top of the hill, executioner Matija Puncer gives his orders, and his assistants pile the bonfire higher.

One hundred eyes follow every movement of their hands.

In the town hall, Judge Krajačić sits waiting for the other judges and talking with Dvojković. The door opens suddenly, and Siniša is standing on the threshold.

'You're not at the burning?' says the Judge.

'Is that why I gained the honour of a captaincy, sir? To attend such an insane horror?'

The opening lines of *Malleus Maleficarum* are classic Zagorka. It's punchy, engaging stuff: a vivid sense of place and action, and the first hints of conflict. The present tense grips: Hilary Mantel would be startling readers with it a century later. It's as brutally efficient as its executioner: the characters are talking, so our understanding is already moving, before we've had to wade through any inert description of anyone. The Judge's first line confirms what's happening, removing the need for any additional narrator intervention and economically setting up the character issue as well. Zagorka tends to speak through an omniscient narrator, but as much as possible uses dialogue to describe events. The first chapter drops you right into the historical atmosphere, rich and dark, and begins to mark out the human tensions. This is writing with a strong feel for the history – its texture, its sensory appeal. It has a skilful command of situation and plot and energy. It knows shrewdly and instinctively what will catch readers. There's no faffing around with dates and archival detail: the reader is immediately immersed in people and drama. It seems, very much, like a journalist's approach to writing.

Gordana opens with a ray of sunlight coming through a castle window and catching a beautiful woman; the subject may be fairy-tale, but that's a cinematographer's eye for how the gaze of the audience must move. The rest of the first paragraph describes the two people in the room, in vivid and romantic terms, again with the immediate sense of conflict. 'They stand reserved, stiff, each keeping their place, as if the narrow space between them is the edge of an abyss. Only their eyes meet like lightning flashes in the darkness of a cloud. And their words roll together like the muffled murmur of an approaching storm.' Again after just the one paragraph of context we're into dialogue: 'Carthage must be destroyed, Lady Isabella, and its prince removed from this world.'

It's fruity stuff, and not to everyone's taste: you have to be susceptible to Croatian national pride and plucky mediaeval heroines and a touch of witchcraft. But it has been, and remains, to many people's taste – especially in Croatia. In recent years she's been informally declared the most widely-read Croatian writer, and a 2005 newspaper poll had her as the second most popular Croat writer ever.

She was popular in both senses of the word. The public read her and were fond of her: she was nicknamed the Enchantress of Grič and the Queen of the Croats. Everyone's grandmother can and will talk about her, and the author as well as her writing are still treated with affection. Generations of Croatian baby girls have been given the names of her heroines. Her novels were serialised, in the Dickensian manner with episodic cliff-hangers, and her public would gather in crowds to snap up the next instalment, and swap chapters to save money. In women's craft workshops, one colleague would be deputed to entertain the rest by reading Zagorka aloud.

Despite her relatively affluent upbringing, she was determinedly of the people. Famously she spent more time with the servants on the aristocratic estate where her father was a manager. She lived out her life in an apartment close to the bustle of the city's central market. Her writing deliberately avoided high-blown literary forms – again, perhaps, the journalism helped – in favour of the language she would have heard in those streets. Zagorka researcher Neda Novosel suggests that 'she brought the audience to the theater, that is, she de-elitised it'. It was natural that she would get involved in film, which began as little more than a fairground attraction and has endured as the most democratic of all the arts. Once she was more established as a novelist, she would fill her mind with images of Zagreb from her long walks and from pictures pinned up around her room, and then sit blindfolded while dictating to a typist the reality she was seeing in her mind. This is why her prose is vivid, and why her Zagreb feels so familiar to her Croatian readers.

Two themes dominate her historical fiction: Croatia's struggle for identity and independence; and women's struggle for approximately the same. The treatment is populist; the conviction behind it is passionate. Zagorka picked out the most decisive and dramatic phases of her nation's history – its mediaeval ebb and flow; its subjection to Habsburg, and thus Hungarian, dominance – and dramatised them with tireless energy and emotion. (This kind of theme is always good copy. Note the prevalence of the Jacobite struggle in historical fiction about Scotland; note Daphne Du Maurier and others using British civil wars royalism; note Lorna Doone and Monmouth's rebellion, Robin Hood and Ivanhoe and Anglo-Saxons living under Norman rule. White Americans have had to locate their foundation myths of individual freedom and folk resilience in the wild west of the nineteenth century – though the baddie might still be the sheriff.) Some critics sneered or complained; others praised among other things her use of archive material – including court records covering the treatment of witches – to ground her stories in historical truth, and specifically Croatian historical truth. Again, perhaps, the journalist's instincts were strong in the novelist.

In parallel with the Croatian national heroics, Zagorka's stories focus on strong heroines – their trials and their triumphs. Sometimes they're royalty; sometimes they're peasants. Sometimes their patriotism is set in a mediaeval world misty with magic; sometimes it's in the sharp political context of the early twentieth century. Consistently, the national and political context is the background for a woman's battle to choose, to act, to love, to be. The heart of the Witch of Grič cycle is Countess Nera, who stirs up trouble for herself by saving young and usually working-class women from being burned as witches; there's at least as much serious sociology as mediaeval melodrama, Zagorka recognising that women accused of witchcraft were surprisingly often those who had frustrated men in one way or another. When the Countess is herself facing death as an alleged witch, she's helped not by a Deus Ex Machina but a Dea, the Empress Maria Theresa. As mediaeval historian and activist Martina Findrik points out, 'Traditionally the good woman is the passive woman and – as in soap operas – the active woman is the negative woman. Zagorka was revolutionary because her women are good and active: they ride horses, fire guns, attack men; they have the mission, with men just helping. That's only changing in films now; imagine reading it 50 or 100 years ago.' Her plots frequently feature women dressing as men, and other subversions of traditional gender rôles; she herself is said to have dressed as a man when carrying messages to protestors against the Hungarian regime in 1903. Sometimes the author's personal trials are very close to the surface of the fiction: *Kći Lotrščaka* ('Daughter of Lotrščak') is about a young woman married off, and how she is declared unsuitable and cast out; *Jadranka* is built around employment as a right and source of independence for a woman; *Kamen na Cesti* ('A Stone on the Road') is essentially autobiographical. Zagorka was writing of women, for women, for all women.

The Habsburg Empire and the reality of its citizens is a bewildering beast to try to capture on paper. (The author asserts from bitter experience that it's even worse trying to do so in fiction, where explanatory paragraphs of elaborate mediaeval geo-politics are not easily interwoven. Zagorka had it easy: she could expect her readers to take it all for granted and jump straight into the beautiful princesses and witch-burning.) Its extent changed over time; its internal boundaries changed over time; the constitutional status and structure of government of its different elements was diverse and, of course, changed over time. The subtleties, fluidities and insecurities of south-eastern European identity – by which a person's citizenship can change several times during one lifetime – are unimaginable to people who, for example, have grown up on an island whose essential borders have not changed in eight thousand years, with the same capital city for much of the last two thousand. Yugoslavia emerged, like a prominence from receding floodwaters, when two empires fell away to north and south of her. Yugoslavia collapsed because the fault lines created by a millennium and a half of migrations and centuries of jostling between those two empires proved more enduring than her few decades of map-making and state-building.

By Zagorka's time, Croats like her endured an uncomfortable double subordination. Putting it over-simply, after the upheavals of revolution and war in nineteenth century Europe, the Empire was split into so-called Austrian and Hungarian halves, with Vienna still the imperial capital but the southern and eastern half of the empire having substantial autonomy and governed from

Budapest. This was a compromise to placate Hungarian national sentiment, but didn't do much for the sentiment of other nationalities. Croatia – with memories of an independent existence as a kingdom centuries earlier, and having helped the Austrians defeat the Hungarians – found itself subordinated to the latter. The chopping and changing of constitutional status was accompanied by more fraught attempts to manage and adjust national identity through policies that promoted or suppressed ethnic groups and languages – for example, Budapest's insistence that only Hungarian be used on the railway signs. All of which is to say: if you marry a proud young Croat to a Hungarian petty official, the latent tensions over breakfast will be considerable.

Such was the context for Zagorka's political journalism – developments in Vienna and Budapest as well as Zagreb were significant for her people – and for her patriotic campaigning. Identity – your sense of who you were and therefore what you felt about the railway signs – could put you on the wrong side of significant political, cultural and administrative developments. Identity could be pride, but it could also be vulnerability. In her student polemics, in her mature articles, in her colourful fictionalisation of historical episodes and in unknowable dinner-table defiances she was fighting not only for the greater freedom of her culture, but for its survival. The inherent seriousness of those mediaeval romances lies in the fact that Zagorka's heroines were fighting essentially the same battles as their author. Her politics could – and did – get her arrested. Her domestic defiance got her certified.

There's an obvious intersectionality to the struggles of a female Croat under the Habsburgs at the beginning of the twentieth century. It illuminates the experience of many women across the region and the centuries, under ever-shifting political geography and persistently patriarchal societies. Did that make Zagorka a more powerful advocate, her status as a woman leaving her more deeply aware of the multi-faceted frustrations of oppression, just as her skills as journalist and novelist reinforced each other? She spoke to Croats, for the rights of Croats, against restriction of their freedoms as such; but her work was hampered because half of her audience were at the same time restricting her freedoms as a woman. The men who championed the cause that she wrote for resisted her right to do so. Was it her rejection of imperial political orthodoxy that got her sent to an asylum, or her rejection of universal gender orthodoxy? Did that confinement as an insufficiently-submissive woman have anything of the proud public worthiness of her imprisonment for inciting patriotic unrest? Habsburg and Hungarian rule disappeared after the First World War, to be replaced by a system that – however volatile and imperfect – gave Croats substantially more political equality and power; Zagorka was still fighting to be read and heard as a woman after the Second World War.

During the long century between the Napoleonic wars and the end of the First World War, the Balkan broth re-congealed into a set of statelets in which 'national' identity was the dominant but never exactly definitive feature. (Indigenous identity powered the state; left-over imperial quirks and new Great Power compromises defined its borders and, thereby, the enduring instabilities of the twentieth century.) For each of the ethnic groups, some kind of cultural re-awakening and flourishing was an essential part of the crystallisation of national identity: the promotion and formalisation of national language; the validation of folk traditions and tales; a burst of creativity, indigenous and so by definition patriotic. Significantly, though, the first generations of these were never entirely pure, never entirely autochthonous. The stimulus and structure for the cultural flourishing – the dictionary, the book of folk-tales, the patriotic poem, the campaigning journalism, the re-telling of the national epic – depended on individuals and on awareness that crossed the borders between the new states and the old external centres of influence. Slav pioneers drew inspiration and support from Vienna and St Petersburg. (Geographically, Zagreb is nearer Vienna, Budapest and Venice than it is to Belgrade and Sarajevo.) Albanian pioneers found external energy everywhere from the Bosphorous to Boston. This is not in any way to diminish the significance or authenticity of the national cultural awakenings. But it is to emphasise that they all emerged in borderlands cultural as well as physical, from a process of cultural exchange and emulation. Bishop Strossmayer's enlightened patronage of Zagorka's journalistic career, and his patriotic encouragement of her historical fiction, does not suggest that the inspiration, integrity, ability and passion were anything other than her own. A very particular individual, she was nonetheless in a particular and transitional time and place.

Does the instinct and agility to innovate – science fiction, film – come from never being allowed to be comfortable with the status quo? Zagorka was perpetually a traveller in physical and psychological borderlands (no man's lands?): the one who came from beyond the hills to Zagreb; the educated daughter of upwardly-mobile parents who spent more time with the servants; the Croat married to a Hungarian, in an Austrian as well as Hungarian empire, and then in a 'Kingdom of Serbs, Croats and Slovenes' and eventually Yugoslavia; the journalist-novelist; the historical romancer who wrote science fiction; the woman in a man's world.

Ana Zbiljski, overseer of the memorial centre based in Zagorka's old apartment, notes that 'she is somehow unfairly perceived as a tragedian, and we can often hear the phrase "Poor Zagorka!". She was everything, just not miserable. She had a fascinating life story. She lived life exactly the way she wanted to. She was free. She has done an indescribable amount for Croatian culture and journalism. Although she did not get the status she deserved from the institutions… she was and remains adored.'

As icon and as voice, Zagorka is still active in the new millennium. The product of nineteenth century traditions and politics, the warrior of the social and cultural battles of the twentieth (and the victim of its endless upheavals, and of the harsh limitations on its notions of equality and liberty), she is still read and heard at the beginning of the twenty-first. She is still popular, and she is still necessary.

At a time when women were becoming a more distinctive section of the reading public and the working public, Zagorka offered them advocacy and arenas for advocacy, romantic icons to inspire them and an individual example to do the same. She lived through the period when the struggle for women's equality – in voting, in the contractual aspects of marriage, in access to employment – moved to the front pages, and she helped to put it there. But despite her particular achievements, and those of many other women, none of those battles was conclusively won in her lifetime.

The cosmopolitan inter-war Yugoslavia of Zagorka's middle-age years, and the brave new world socialist Yugoslavia she saw before her death, remained socially conservative – too often distracted by disputed versions of national liberation, and overlooking individual liberation. As a side-note on how women's power to communicate was policed – and on how married women were policed – an 1888 Austro-Hungarian law had required celibacy for women teachers, and a 1937 measure suggested that a woman should give up teaching if she married. The women's union Zagorka founded in 1897 was banned not for its political provocativeness, but for 'immorality'. There were limits to the ambitions of some feminists, and limitations to what they could achieve. In an analysis of women's magazines in neighbouring Serbia just before it became part of a federation with Croatia, Ana Kolarić describes how a 'curious amalgam of emancipatory and patriarchal discourses... resulted in a specific notion of proper womanly behaviour. ... Woman's main purpose is to remain a woman. Educated and equal, but woman.' This links to a similarly dubious model of patriotism which has been too prevalent in south-eastern Europe and elsewhere: emancipation was to make woman a more effective patriot, and the fundamental patriotic duty of woman was to breed (and then raise her children with wholesome cooking and wholesome ideals). As late as the 1990s, Serbian women were being criticised – see for example the governing party's 1992 'Warning on the Demographic Movements of the Serbian Population' – for their progressiveness specifically because it was allegedly leading them to produce fewer children than the supposedly more submissive and traditional Albanians.

Women secured their right to vote in Austria, and to a considerable extent Hungary, in 1918; in Zagorka's Yugoslavia they had to wait until 1945. The political remnants of Croatian nationalism – responsible in the 1990s for independence from Yugoslavia and for war crimes – tend to survive now in an informal right-wing coalition with social conservatives, who also capitalise on the enduring power of the Catholic church in the country. Campaigners point to weak protection for representation of women in parliament, and weak results (often lower than in Communist times). Abortion is legal only until ten weeks, and even that provision has come under pressure; medical staff are in any case entitled by law to object to carrying out an abortion. There were public protests in 2018 opposing Croatia's ratification of the Istanbul Convention on violence against women.

In Autumn 2020, Croatia and her former Yugoslav neighbours marked the 75th anniversary of women's suffrage. Celebrants noted how they'd really had to fight for the right: the artist who produced portraits of all 91 women to win Yugoslavia's highest award for military valour noted that more than 100,000 Yugoslav women had fought for the anti-fascist resistance, and more than a quarter of those had died in the fighting. But activists found themselves in an internet spat over relative freedoms: right-wing commentators belittled both the achievement and its commemoration on the grounds that it happened under communism. Perhaps if you believe you exist within a purely national framework, then it becomes possible to identify a hierarchy of freedoms within it – better for Croats to be free of Yugoslavia, than for women to be free in it. By contrast, women in Croatia seemed to feel that their rights and identities as women were distinct from and even transcended their rights and identities as Croats: 'women's right to vote in Yugoslavia wasn't only about elections, but about the wider rôle of women in society, institutions and political structures'; and (from a male commentator) 'women fought for the right to vote and with it they gained equality with men. That's the point. They won that right, whatever system it was in.' (Virginia Woolf thought patriotism actually incompatible with being a woman, writing in *Three Guineas* in 1938, 'As a woman, I have no country. As a woman I want no country. As a woman my country is the whole world.')

Zagorka's apartment was eventually acquired by the Centre for Women's Studies, and transformed into an engine of cultural activity, scholarship and activism. Marija Jurić Zagorka Days have been held annually in her honour, highlighting enduring unresolved challenges to women's equality. The announcement of one recent iteration noted that, 'With the economic crisis and the disintegration of the welfare state in recent decades, we are witnessing increased neo-liberalisation of the media and public goods, the re-traditionalisation of public institutions and conservative attacks on women's rights'.

Her brand is still strong – as woman, as pioneer, as prominent cultural figure. On International Women's Day recently, the British Ambassador to Croatia published an imaginary letter from Agatha Christie to Marija Jurić Zagorka, linking their struggles – failed first marriages, the abusive assertions of mental illness – and eventual enduring triumph. (Agatha Christie was perhaps the closest British equivalent to Zagorka in terms of the number of people who read her, and the way they read her.) Zagorka's passion and endurance speak a century later, her cause still unrealised, her sufferings still lived by many women.

Remarkably, her historical fiction speaks too. Her novels are still available on Kindle, cheaply and easily accessible to much the same audience she satisfied so successfully back then. Her style is still very effective – more so than that of officially distinguished contemporaries. By one recent analysis, her popularity is yet again resurgent in the context of the popularity of young adult and/or gothic romance novels. The covers of the modern editions are not what you'd expect on century-old literature: they have air-brushed fantasy women, darkly beautiful among their mysteries. On the cover of one of the Gordana books, the heroine stands at bay brandishing her sword; her elegant gown constrains her legs, rather impractically, and fails to constrain her breasts; the arms of a dozen unseen men reach for her. The bound woman advertising *Mala Revolucionarka Roblje* ('Young Revolutionary Slave') is pure *Fifty Shades*. We've come a long way from the dumpy matron of the statue, from the umbrella to the sword, but it's an indication of Zagorka's vision: she was writing of a world, for a world, far beyond her own.

The fact that her memory is so alive in modern Croatia, an icon of feminist advocacy as much as tourist interest, is a nice testament to her abilities but a more sobering reflection of the extent of her achievement. If only it were possible to consign her to cosy statuesque memory, to romantic fictionalisations. Instead she must work on, a medium for activist scholarship and campaigning initiatives and advocacy days and internet articles.

Perhaps it is the ambiguity of her image – the radical pioneer disguised as a grandmother – that has made her so enduringly powerful. That statue is a fair picture of how most Croats see her: the beloved old matron of popular literature. But in reading her and remembering her for her familiar easy-listening virtues, consciously or sub-consciously they absorb less cosy ideas. Martina Findrik suggests that though Zagorka herself would have believed her journalism the most important part of her work, it's her other writing that has the enduring impact. 'Feminism often has a negative label; it's always politically associated. But people are happier to associate with her; saying that she was a feminist makes it more palatable. Zagorka is Zagorka. You may be on the left, you may be on the right: she's the connection point. Zagorka triggers an emotional memory.'

There was to be no comfortable retirement for Marija Jurić Zagorka, no genteel retreat, no stately decline. Unlike so many male literary heroes, she never won the easy veneration of her society. Her last years were lonelier, harder. Hers was a pathetic, even tragic ending, an uncomfortable minor key, far from the splendid conclusions of fiction. But perhaps this is consistent with the reality of a life fighting on the front line. Hers was never a settled life, never entirely comfortable, never entirely conventional. And her work – her cause, her influence – isn't settled either. Like the deceptively old-fashioned statue, Zagorka is still moving.

Chapter 3

Finding Xenia: the Montenegrin photographer princess

> "A man, when he undertakes a journey, has, in
> general the end in view; a woman thinks more of
> the incidental occurrences, the strange things that
> may possibly occur on the road"
> Mary Wollstonecraft, *A Vindication of the Rights
> of Women*

I was standing in a bedroom which seemed to be having an identity crisis. The bed was ornate – black and gilt, and inlaid with mother-of-pearl around the headboard. There was a lavish burlesque quality to it, and yet it was a single bed. And it stood on a bare parquet floor which would be decidedly cool to the touch of a toe in winter here in Montenegro. On the wall was an icon. Could one use the word 'monastic' of a room where even the wardrobe was winking mother-of-pearl at me?

In one corner there was a nightstand (more mother-of-pearl, more gilt) which held a Bennet typewriter and an old Kodak camera; the burgundy velvet folds of its concertina extended, as if it were focusing on a very small detail, or something far away.

I was in Cetinje, Montenegro's former capital that British writer William Le Queux described in 1907 as 'a little city in the sky'. His contemporary, Edith Durham, described it as the 'oddest toy capital conceivable' and there was certainly something Liliputian, and maybe even Ruritanian about the town I'd come to visit. The country was created in 1878 and ruled first by Prince Nikola, who was only crowned king in 1910 (he fled to exile in 1916). With the emergence of this new regional player, embassies began to be sent out. When Montenegro was born, Cetinje didn't even have a hotel, but soon the town perched on the karst was receiving a disproportionate number of foreigners, each with a modest embassy building. The result was a town which today still has a population of only 17,000 but certainly has pretensions. Including a palace, in which I was standing.

King Nikola, whose palace this was, was known as the 'father-in-law of Europe' for the skilful matchmaking he contrived for his daughters who were successfully married into the royal houses of Bulgaria, Germany, Italy, Russia, and Serbia. But the tour guide showing us round the palace said that Nikola's eighth daughter was different. 'Xenia never married,' she told us. 'Instead she became a secretary and advisor to her father,' – she gestured at the typewriter, and then at the other equipment on display. 'And she was a passionate photographer. She learned to drive, and was the first woman in Montenegro to do so. That meant she was independent and could drive out to take pictures of her country.'

We moved on from Xenia's bedroom and into the other rooms of the palace, and then out into the town and off on the rest of our Balkan itinerary, but the image of that room stayed with me, with its contradictions and its brave choices. Xenia was intriguing and inspiring and I wanted to find out more about her.

It took four years before I had the chance to return to Cetinje and learn more about Xenia there. In the meantime I tried online research which turned up depressingly little apart from a vivid account in the *Newburgh Telegram* of Xenia's marriage proposal from Alexander I of Serbia,

'In he shambled, grinning, blinking, through his heavy glasses, knock-kneed, and most unattractive. The princess gave him one glance and shuddered.

"Mon Dieu!" she cried in French, *"mais vous êtes impossible!"* or in polite English, she frankly told Alexander that he was impossible. It was the cry of an innocent, unspoiled young girl. The Prince was not at all rebuffed, and attempted to mumble some protest that perhaps fatigue and nervousness had overcome Her Royal Highness.

Xenia gasped once more. And then she fled from the room. The royal romance had died before it was born. Alexander married Mme Draga Maschin, and a few years later both were assassinated by the King's officers in the royal palace at Belgrade.'

A lucky escape for Xenia then – but I wondered what her life had been like after taking that bold stance against the 'father-in-law of Europe'. I did discover that it was not the only time – a decade later, Xenia joined some anti-Austrian protests in Cetinje which led to calls from Nikola's Austrian allies for sanctions against her. The King obligingly exiled his daughter, but the place she was banished to was Paris. I wasn't sure how grave a punishment that might have seemed to any of those involved.

I turned my online research to focus on available accommodation in Cetinje, and having contacted the National Library of Montenegro to ask if I could consult their Xenia holdings, I made it back.

When I arrived in town this time, I found the building that was marked as the library in the former French Embassy (completed 1910). However, when I got inside it was explained that this was just one department of the library and for my enquiry I was directed to the main collection – 'the former Italian Embassy', said the librarian helpfully – and as I navigated the streets it felt more like I was seeking asylum than researching a royal past.

When I finally got seated in the next former embassy, and I started reading, I wondered whether my reference to asylum was in fact an appropriate image. Maybe Xenia had really had to make a tour of these embassies in the uncertain months of 1916 before her family fled into exile with the arrival of a joint Austro-Hungarian, German and Bulgarian force in their country. Xenia ended up in France, with her sister and the King and Queen, and she lived there for the rest of her life. I guessed her journey there would have started by boat across the Adriatic to Italy so perhaps the staff of this building a century before had been important gatekeepers on her flight to safety.

The Italians' former embassy was completed the same year as that of the French. It was set in trees and had the atmosphere of a sanatorium. Inside we were in a well-heated room with high ceilings and velvet curtains the colour of foxed manuscripts. Desks all faced the front, like in an exam room, and the floor creaked whenever I moved – it was a place to be still. And everywhere there was old-fashioned courtesy – as if the place was still peopled with early twentieth century diplomats. When I had trouble deciphering the elaborate Cyrillic on a sign in one of Xenia's photos and asked a librarian for help, she then asked one of the readers, and suddenly we were all on the same team, all facing the same way – historians versus the past; readers versus the illegible, researchers versus the inscrutable.

The book I was trying to make sense of was a collection of Xenia's photographs. Now out of print, it had been impossible to find outside Montenegro. Its pages reflected the same identity crisis I had seen a hint of in her bedroom; on the one hand there was the opening of a golf club, tennis, garden parties. Like Renoir's paintings, in many shots there were more parasols visible than people. But there were also fishermen, a cook who could only just be seen through the steam of his pot, a Marquis picking flowers in the mountains: the behind-the-scenes snapshots of real life for all classes. There were many photos, but I searched through them almost in vain for the clues to what I was really looking for... the one person who didn't feature there, because it was she who was taking them. Of course in some ways this was the closest I could possibly get to her: getting almost literally inside her head, to see what her eyes saw. But ultimately it was frustrating.

What I did catch of her came in words rather than in images. The book quoted Xenia's contemporary, Dušan

Balšić saying of her 'she is a courageous and skilled shot with a pistol or a gun'. It also included lines from a letter she wrote where she described herself, 'I believe that I have a good-tempered nature, however I can flare up in an outpouring of fury; on such an occasion, the detractor had better not come my way. He would learn what Montenegrin revenge means, and it is not a myth.'

Eventually I did find some photographs of her and tried to bring them to life. She had strong, determined features: I bet she could have been stubborn; maybe even imperious. Certainly quite frightening when furious. A contemporary newspaper ran an article entitled 'Pretty Princesses: The Crop of Royal Brides in Europe' where they wrote 'Princess Xenia is now twenty-one years of age and a brunette beauty of semi-Oriental type'. But the newspaper was *The New Zealand Star* and I realised that they were presumably only going on the same photographs I was, such are the distances of time and space – and the narrowing of them by cyberspace.

From the library I returned to the palace. I went back to look at that conflicted bedroom, filling it now with more of what I'd learned about Xenia from my reading and the glimpses of her life.

'Oh, she was smart – she knew so many languages' said the woman working in the museum gift shop when I told her I was trying to find out more about Xenia. Me with my broken Serbian and she with no English nodded in appreciation of Xenia's linguistic ability. 'And you can really tell how clever she was,' she added, 'from the fact that she never got married.'

We chatted some more and exchanged names. She told me that there were primary sources I should consult if I really wanted to learn more about Xenia, including correspondence held at the National Library. I needed to spend more time on this quest, but there were no days left on this trip.

It was another five months before I could return, bouncing back to Cetinje in buses and taxis over the mountain roads from where I was living in Albania. I recognised the irony of me, a woman who is an unconfident driver, hoping to find Xenia on trips when I was dependent on someone else at the wheel. I was starting to imagine the way Xenia would have looked at me, part supercilious, part simply uncomprehending.

For this third visit I arrived in Cetinje when there was still snow piled along the pavements, and the steady drip of the thaw from guttering. The snow was starting to pit, to sully, to morph into new shapes like garbage left out too long. I saw a dead and soggy rat. But I pressed on, remembering another line from William Le Queux,

> 'A good many foreigners come up from Cattaro [modern-day Kotor, the town on the coast that is now Montenegro's cruise-ship capital] to pry about Cetinje for a day or two, buy picture-postcards and antique arms, sneer at the honest Montenegrin, and return into Dalmatia. Towards such, the Montenegrin is not particularly polite. But those who go to Cetinje to seriously and thoroughly study the people and their future will find a great deal of genuine and charming hospitality.'

For the practicalities of hospitality I was relying on Airbnb but it didn't start well. I had no replies to my SMS and emails asking for exact directions to find my apartment. As I wandered the streets surrounding the pin on the Google map showing on my phone, I lost the final drips of its battery. Without that I was truly lost.

I asked an old lady looking out from her hallway into the street – had she heard of the apartment name? No. But along came a good-looking teenage boy who seemed to be her grandson. '*Da li imaš* smartphone?' I asked him. He said he didn't have one, but with impressive commitment to the 'charming hospitality' I'd been told about, he went into the house and came out with an iPhone that apparently belonged to his mum. Together we tried navigating its different languages and settings and eventually I was able to find a message from my Airbnb host who drove to find me and brought me to his apartment.

The next morning I'd arranged to meet with a translator, Marko, and we went back to the former Embassy where I'd ordered boxes of Xenia's correspondence to read. These were from the archives of the Legate, Pero Šoć, who corresponded with Xenia in exile. Marko and I each took up fistfuls of letters.

Paper turns like skin with age – greasy and then softening and becoming brittle – and there was a story told even from the textures and colours of the documents we handled. Pero Šoć wrote on paper reminiscent of school toilet paper. ('Oh, he's having problems again with his rent…' commented Marko, reading to me from the Cyrillic. I wondered whether Xenia had a secretary doing the same thing for her when these letters arrived).

Xenia was not apparently forced to such economies, and I remembered a 1924 article I'd found in the Times about the closing down of the Montenegrin Relief Fund, after ten years. 'About £80,000 in all was collected, [the modern day equivalent would be about £24 million] and many thousands of destitute Montenegrin refugees were helped, including a member of the late King's family.'

Amongst the documents, we started to recognise Xenia's beautiful envelopes, with violet or moss-green tissue paper inside – and purchased with who-knew-what funding. We noted the black edging to letters, too, as she reeled from family bereavement to bereavement – in 1918 her older brother Mirko died aged just 39, in 1921 her beloved father, in 1923 her mother; in 1927 the sister – Vjera – to whom she was closest died aged 40. Five years later, her younger brother, Petar, died aged 42; three years after that came the death of her elder sister who had been with her in Antibes.

I learned to recognise, too, Xenia's large, dramatic handwriting – I imagined her writing fast and fluently. Where there were words she wanted to add in, she did so with a swooping line.

But the quality of her notepaper started to deteriorate. In April 1925 she lamented 'I have been waiting for four and a half years for my affairs to be sorted out, without being able to touch a centime.' By June she was writing that she was obliged to rent out their villa and that they were leaving in five days. In September there was the news that they had sold their house in Constantinople.

The life in exile was melancholy and also apparently without illustration. I had found no more photographs by Xenia from when she left for exile. Was it her state of mind that had changed irrevocably? Or had it only been the imperative of presenting Montenegro to the world that had prompted her to seek out the images I'd seen? She lived until 1960, through many generations of new photographic development – which I could find no proof that she had ever touched.

I wanted to be reminded of Xenia the explorer of her country, of new technology – the young woman rattling around the Montenegrin countryside with car and camera. So I went back to the palace.

The woman who came to open the door to the palace was familiar from my last visit. I even dragged her name from my memory; her eyebrows shot up when I greeted her as Sanja, and it was with a friendly smile that she took me down to the offices in the basement to introduce me to the Director, Tatjana Jović, and Andje Kapičić, the author of the book of photographs I'd enjoyed at the National Library.

It was an intimidating audience, especially when I had such inadequate language skills to talk to them. I knew so little about someone they had both studied for years; I had nothing to offer them and was dependent on their goodwill in giving me any of their time or sharing expertise. I smiled hopefully at them both. I'd been promised an interpreter, but before she arrived, another woman came in. Maja was Andje's daughter, and the person through whom I'd been communicating about this meeting

'I don't have a computer or any of that,' Andje said, in explanation of why it was Maja whom I'd had to email. 'Just a typewriter'.

'Like Xenia,' I commented, remembering the machine I'd seen four years ago when I'd first heard about the Princess. But now, having read Xenia's correspondence I bet she would have used Facebook if it had been available.

Maja had her five-year-old son with her and he and I tried to exchange some English, though it mainly consisted of him counting up to 12 and then leaving the room with a cheery wave and the unsettling farewell, 'Good luck!' I didn't know whether it was a mistake or a warning.

Sanja saved me. She told the other women about my previous visit – 'She even remembered my name,' and so I explained to her, and the other women in the room, the reason she had stuck in my mind.

'When I was talking to you in the museum bookshop on my last visit, you said to me that we could tell that Princess Xenia was clever, not just because she could speak three foreign languages, but also because she never married!'

The room erupted in the laughter of female solidarity. This meeting was going to be OK.

I was offered more hospitality, in the form of tea. A cup was brought in for me but it was put on the table so close to the album of Xenia's original photographs that had been set out for me to look at that I was too scared to drink; too scared that in lifting it to my mouth I would slop liquid over the priceless images.

Andje had started talking as soon as I had sat down, despite the fact that the interpreter hadn't arrived yet, and I could only understand half of what she was saying. She was an elegant woman in a black leather skirt with a beautiful face with bones like Katherine Hepburn. She wanted to know whether I had particular questions, which was frustrating because I knew enough Serbian to understand what she was offering me, but not enough to ask any of the questions I had bubbling inside me.

Once Ana, the interpreter, arrived, I could set my questions free. Could they tell me about Xenia's education? Yes, she had had private, foreign tutors, at least one of them Swiss, at the palace in Cetinje. She and Vjera had been able to take their exams at the Girls' Institute which had recently opened in Cetinje.

And what about the School for Women that I'd read about being founded 'under Xenia's auspices'? I got out an article from an in-flight magazine where I had read about the school on an aeroplane to Montenegro some years ago, to show them what I was talking about. Only as I did so did I notice a name in the article – Tatjana Jović. I showed it to her and she flickered with pride before hurrying out of the room calling back over her shoulder, 'I'm going to get you a present.'

She came back with the heavy illustrated catalogue of the exhibition she had curated.

I moved the perilous cup of tea well out of the way so I could look properly at the book, and when I'd finished I also finally felt confident to open up Xenia's album. There were about three hundred of her photographs, each with its negative, though I didn't take those out of their little greaseproof-paper envelopes, like After Eight mints.

I could look carefully at Xenia's images of her mother – a woman who started childbearing at the age of 16 and continued with twelve children, until the age of 41. She looked strong.

The images revealed details of her outfits which hinted at another kind of identity crisis. I had read from William le Queux that the King had mandated all Montenegrins to wear traditional dress, with the only exemptions being for members of the court. I could only wonder at the reasons for this – aspiring to the values of Montenegro's martial medieval past? A way to increase the status of court members (and his marriageable daughters) by allowing them to float in Parisian lace and couture while other women sweltered in homespun?

The photographs suggested that Queen Milena had not felt completely sure of such an edict. Certainly, she was wearing a long pale blouse whose rows of delicate lacework at placket, cuff and collar were not part of traditional Montenegrin costume. However, as my attention ranged along the hem's fine needlework I realised that below the long blouse, the distinctive bird's wing embroidery of the traditional *zubun* sleeveless housecoat was visible. Looking closer it was evident that Queen Milena was in fact wearing traditional dress with her flimsy imported outer garment hastily snatched up on top. Was this for the benefit of her daughter's photograph? Or was the compromise one she wore every day, keeping her heritage close to her skin?

Other photographs similarly repaid close scrutiny. For example, in one picture, Xenia had captured fishermen bent double over their nets; the shape of their backs echoed in the livestock we can see in the field beyond the lake. In another, they haul in a net – the textures gorgeous as the camera captures the ripple of muscles in their backs, the folds of material in their baggy loincloths, the seine just sitting on the surface of the water, and the hills rippling similarly in the background.

I told the women who'd been sitting watching me that I'd like to take some photographs of them as a memento of our meeting. Everyone did what women do in such circumstances, smoothing skirts, pulling in stomachs, snapping elastic into place. They took up position against a wall where a reproduction of King Nikola's portrait stared down at us. His mouth was slightly puckered as if he was a little disappointed. I got my shot, but I also got a strong sense of the experience Xenia would have had taking photographs under the same stern gaze. I remembered that the striking image of the King that Andje had chosen for the cover of her book of Xenia's photographs was of Nikola's back.

On the one hand, it's an intimate picture possible only with the proximity that a daughter or other close family member would be allowed. With the Montenegrin landscape visible over the King's shoulder, it's also a dramatic picture of a sovereign gazing out across his domain. But it's a photograph that reinforces distance – not only in the monarch who's turned his back on his daughter, but one whose head can't even be seen. Another parasol (or, more likely, given Cetinje's famously prodigious rainfall, an umbrella) is being held by the King to shield him from the weather, making a composition which has the obscured features of a Magritte.

We looked a little longer at the images together and I had a chance to appreciate more details, like in an unremarkable photograph of the Italian envoy, Luigi Cusani Confalonieri, shown standing with Xenia's sister-in-law by a river on a sunny day. What distinguished the picture was the shadow showing at the bottom of the image – the shape of the photographer's tam o'shanter-style hat clearly visible. It's the closest to a selfie we can get to see, given the limited technology available to Xenia.

I had had some tantalising glimpses of this woman from my meeting at the museum, but I was still not sure I had got to know her. What made her take those tough decisions? To push back against being married off in advantageous royal alliance? To turn her back on the traditional roles of wife and mother that were expected of her, and which left her in lonely exile in France for her last years? Even to advise her father against his politically savvy connection with the Austrians? For a woman whose name came from the Greek word, ξενία, for 'hospitality' I wondered how much safe quarter she had been able to find in a vagabond life.

I left the museum to get back to the Airbnb apartment where I'd left my bag. The roads didn't look familiar and I soon started seeing shops selling plastic flowers. That means death, and sure enough, shortly afterwards I saw a cemetery, which I knew I'd not passed in the journey from the apartment in the morning. I retraced my steps and tried a road running parallel on the other side. It took me to a modern housing estate and I knew that wasn't right either. A white-haired man was just going into his house and I called out to him in my beginner's Montenegrin,

'Excuse me?' I repeated the name of the road where my apartment was.

He asked why I was going there, and I got out the words for 'my apartment'.

He laughed; not unkindly but not briefly either.

'You're lost?' he guffawed. 'On the way to your apartment?' He really couldn't believe it.

'Well, yes,' I said, and started to laugh myself now.

'Wait here,' he gestured, and went into his house (why? to get a map? To shut the door and never come out?). He was still laughing at me when he turned back and beckoned me in. 'My wife,' he said in a sort of explanation.

Inside was a woman who said I should call her Georgina and whom I later discovered was 66 but who looked much younger. Her husband told her I was lost on the way to my apartment and she smiled too. I was sat down (protesting in an English way) and given an enormous glass of blueberry juice. 'Don't worry, we have a toilet', said the practical couple when they saw my otherwise inexplicable reluctance to have a cool drink on a hot day in the middle of a long walk. Then they proposed food and I protested again – I needed to get to my apartment, pick up my bag and get to Podgorica.

They switched to English.

'Slow down,' said Bojo (pronounced 'Boyo' and thus incongruously Welsh, though with his small stature and ease with himself he did remind me of some of the best Welshmen I've known).

'Thank you,' I smiled, adding, 'your English is excellent.'

'Excellent like me,' he laughed, for almost as long as he had at the idea of me being lost.

'Is that true?' I asked his wife, who raised an eyebrow and we all started to make friends.

Bojo had been in the merchant navy for forty years. He told me about his stay in 'Glasgov' where he said he'd found the Scots friendly but couldn't handle the way they drank.

'Men and women too. Men drink, OK; but women…?' I wondered how Xenia would have replied.

He said that he had spent most of his time at sea. Later, when he took credit for his wife's young looks – 'it's because of me!' – I felt I knew him, and their dynamic, well enough to comment.

'Yes, it's because of you – being away all the time.' It got the largest laugh of all – from both of them.

They asked about the heavy coffee-table books I was carrying which were presents from the women I'd met at the museum, and I told them about my conversation with Andje and Tatjana and how helpful they'd been with my research. They knew the women, reminding me that Cetinje is a small town. Not quite as small as it had been in Xenia's day – I had read that in the 1860 census it had just 34 households. A bold place for King Nikola to designate as capital of his new kingdom. Even by 1910 – when construction had finished on all the former Embassy buildings and palaces I'd seen on my visit, and the town had the trappings of a centre of power – the census recorded it as the world's smallest capital with just 5,895 inhabitants. With three times that today, it still seemed that everyone knew all about one another.

'Andje's divorced,' Bojo said.

'And Tatjana never married,' said Georgina.

I thought again about the laughter there had been from the women at the museum at their colleague's witticism on us knowing how smart Xenia had been not just because she knew so many languages, 'but because she never married.'

My audiobook for the bus journey here had been Mary Wollstonecraft's *A Vindication of the rights of Women*. She quotes Bacon, 'the best works, and of greatest merit for the public, have proceeded from the unmarried or childless men' and comments 'I say the same of women.'

Georgina and Bojo served me Plazma biscuits – rusks made for babies but beloved as comfort food across the former Yugoslavia – and then Georgina got out a box of chocolate bars. There were three and I thought how kind of her to offer one to each of us. But no, they were all for me to take with me. She really brooked no argument.

'I'm going to get fat!' I said. 'But it's worth it for those delicious Plazma biscuits…' Such comments are dangerous in houses like these – before I could say more, Georgina was in the pantry and taking out an unopened packet of Plazma. These also were all for me.

I thanked them profusely.

And, er, could they now tell me the way to the street of my apartment?

'No, no!'

Bojo would drive me.

'And are you just picking up your bag there before setting off to Podgorica? If so, I'll then drive you on to the bus station.'

'If you're going to do something, do it properly,' said Bojo as I was bundled into his car.

Exploring this town's architectural, photographic and museum heritage, I had some beautiful insights into Xenia herself, but here I had also stumbled on some deep and powerful sources of the ξενία for which she was named.

Chapter 4

Maga Magazinović:
'Is there a profession women are not capable of?'

'I want to go to the National Library,' I said proudly to the Belgrade taxi driver. 'Narodni Biblioteka' I repeated.

He was unimpressed. 'NarodNA Biblioteka,' he corrected my adjectival ending, adding in English, 'is woman!'

The word might be feminine, but as we drew up to my destination I felt that my instinctive assigning of masculine gender to this austere building was understandable. Behind it rose the vast breast of the domed Sveti Sava memorial church, but the library's *pilotis* and reinforced concrete were unrelentingly linear.

Its staff had been just as unrelentingly masculine until 1904 when a 21-year-old girl challenged some of those patriarchal lines. I had come to the library to find out about Maga Magazinović, who combined the distinctions of being the first woman to work in Serbia's library, the first woman to graduate from Belgrade University's Faculty of Philosophy, Serbia's first woman journalist, and the first to bring modern dance, as inspired by Isadora Duncan, to this country.

I jumped out of the cab, as light on my feet as I imagined a dancing librarian would be, and ascended the library steps to begin my quest.

On the lookout for the patriarchy I noted that the first library employee I met – the cloakroom attendant – was a woman. So was the receptionist who guided me to the correct floor where I could research Maga's life. So, indeed, was the librarian in the reading room. When I was shown through to her colleague, also a woman, for help in finding works on Maga's life, I ventured to ask the question.

'Yes, the majority of us at the library now are women,' she confirmed.

Maga opened this and many more doors as she lobbied and argued and danced her way through the barriers to full participation in the labour market and the intellectual life of Belgrade.

The challenge of such achievements by a girl from a working-class family from the Serbian provinces at the turn of the twentieth century should not be underestimated. Maga had been born in Užice, more than two hundred kilometres from the capital and I had first encountered her there, on a visit one year previous to this Belgrade trip. I had been travelling on the Bar to Belgrade railway – often mentioned in lists of the great railway journeys of Europe. I had not made the journey on Tito's famous Blue Train but the reasons for the route's popularity were obvious as we had pulled out of the town of Bar in Montenegro and headed into countryside with stunning mountain views on our right and the sparkling azure of the sea on our left. My zoom lens had stuck its nose out of the windows first on one side of the train and then the other, and then back again, not knowing where to put itself. It had been an enchanting journey for me and for my sister who was travelling with me.

Not so much for her three-year-old son, Alexander, despite the fact that he was already a seasoned traveller with a repertoire of games you could play on the move, a snuggly travel blanket, an iPad and a toy train given to him by his grandmother especially for this trip. All this scenery was a bit much. He could muster up far more excitement – and considerable decibels – for TUNNELLLLLLLLS which he greeted with a gasp at their enveloping darkness, a chuckle at how they blotted out all that Scenery that was taking everyone's attention, how they whipped at your hair and threw dust in your eyes.

And there are 254 tunnels between Bar and Belgrade.

But it had become clear that even these might not be enough to keep Alexander's attention so we had decided to stop for the night in Užice and continue to Belgrade the following day. We'd found an Airbnb, Alexander had gone into the bathroom, worked out how to use the key to lock it, and then failed to work out how to use it to get out. After what felt like an eternity of coaching through the keyhole, and he was out, we had all needed to find a playpark.

We had hastily read up about the city and discovered that in the centre – and not far from both the truly excellent playpark, and the glorious ugliness, Mick Jagger-like, of the Brutalist Hotel Zlatibor – was a municipal car park with murals depicting what I presumed were the town's famous sons, none of whom I recognised. Among them was one famous daughter. The mural was perhaps three metres high and Maga's face was distorted. Maybe I wasn't standing in the right place to see it, or maybe the painter hadn't been, but her face still smiled enigmatically at me over the boot of a Volkswagen Passat. It was then that I started researching who she was, and why she might be smiling.

I learned that she was born in this town in 1882 though when she was a teenager her family moved from Užice to Belgrade where she finished her education. After three years teaching at the girls' high school she went to the University of Berlin. In Germany she studied art history but also learned modern dance with Isadora Duncan and it was there that she met her future husband, Gerhard Gesemann.

So I had the basic biography. As I tapped at the terminal in the National Library and scrolled through its catalogue I learned that the legal environment in Serbia was more supportive of women's power than many other European countries at the time – by a Karadjordje law, for example, dating from the Serbian revolution (1804-1815) a woman who became head of her family had the right and obligation to participate in local assemblies and to discuss all issues. When a decision was to be made, her vote was worth as much as the vote of any man.

A book by Vera Obradović offered two other titbits of context along with a full account of Maga's work and impact which forms the basis of my account here. Apparently Maga's mother, Stana, had a party trick of bending down and taking a ring off her toe with her teeth. Not in itself enough to set a daughter on a course to open a school of modern dance, perhaps, but it's a powerful image.

Combine that with two developments in social and educational policy in late nineteenth century Serbia, and the steady gaze and set jaw I'd seen in the mural might just be enough to create a revolutionary librarian, writer and dancer.

The first of the social developments was the passing of a significant law on education in the year that Maga was born. Stojan Novaković's law made six years of education compulsory for both boys and girls.

The second development at national level which shaped young Maga's life was the closure of co-educational schools in 1896, the year she turned fourteen. Girls were transferred to the High School for Girls in Belgrade, and this was one of the reasons that Maga's family moved from Užice.

Once she was in Belgrade, a third, much more local, policy set the scene, quite literally, for her later passions. She had always been interested in the theatre and wrote how her house in Užice had been next door to an inn which hosted plays by touring theatre companies which she would watch through the fence. But now in Belgrade her father got work as a craftsman at the National Theatre, and a perk of his job was that Maga was allowed to watch performances from the third gallery on Sundays.

Later she wrote in her autobiography her conclusions about the theatre – 'In acting you always give yourself to another person. In dance you mainly express yourself'. Nevertheless, the ambitions of the theatre stayed with her, enough for it still to hurt when she narrated the response to her dream of directing a Shakespeare play at the National Theatre,

'Good God, girl, what are you thinking! You – to direct …?! Even if you had learned from Shakespeare himself …

it is im-poss-i-ble! To be an actress – maybe! But a director! Ha ha ha!'.

I had been excited to think that this remarkable life had played out here but now, looking round the National Library building with its distinctive 1970s architecture, I realised that this could not have been the place where Maga had worked. It turned out that the library had, in her day, been housed in what is now the university rectorate so I left the computer catalogue to find a cab, thinking that en route to the old library I could see another Belgrade site I was particularly keen to visit…

'*Ulica* Mage Magazinović,' I instructed the driver. I had read that a street name in a Belgrade suburb represents one part of this extraordinary woman's legacy.

The homage was slightly undermined by the fact that the driver hadn't heard of the street. Not only that, but when he radioed to the base to ask for instructions he told them he was looking for 'Zage Magazinović' street. He had apparently not heard of the woman either.

'MMMaga,' I murmured at him.

We got talking after that about who this woman was. He said he was trained in pedagogy but he didn't recognise the name of this Serbian teacher.

He told me my Serbian was 'not good but cute' and then he said I had nice eyes. I felt sure that Maga would have known what to do to put him in his place. I tried her steady gaze out of the windscreen.

We found her road eventually – a street of geraniums and unpretentious houses; I don't know whether she would have felt at home here – I've not been able to find out much about her domestic arrangements, except for the plea in a

1925 article for her to have a proper space where she could rehearse her pupils,

'it is necessary … to really help her find and secure at least one classroom to begin with. She usually works in her cramped apartment, and before every class she has to remove the furniture to make space.'

I walked the street reverently, took some photographs, and thought about the grace and drive – the particular mixture of strength and flexibility – needed to be a pioneer of women's dance, of women's work, of the ways that women's bodies and brains are perceived.

Back in the car, I asked the driver to take me to the Captain Miša Building which had been the National Library when Maga had worked there. We wound through traffic and past the Cathedral. The driver crossed himself busily, a total of three times. I wondered at the strange ways people focus their faith, until realising that we were on our way from visiting a road named after a woman who'd inspired me: a trip made just so I could feel I'd been where her name was written up on a signpost.

I walked the last section of the route to the Captain Miša building, past the buzzing cafes of the Kalemegdan – Belgrade's ancient fortress whose name comes from the Turkish for 'Fortress Field'. It's a natural place for a fortress, the nose of land at the confluence of two great rivers. Here you feel your place in the heart of Europe: where the continent's second longest river, the Danube, meets the Sava which has flowed here over 990 kilometres to join two other national capitals – Ljubljana and Zagreb – to this great Serbian city. The Danube itself has passed through three other capitals (Vienna, Bratislava and

Budapest) to get here, thus holding the world record for the number of capital cities joined by any river, as well as for the number of countries (ten) which it flows through on its 2850km journey to the Black Sea. Watching it flow by you are reminded that the Danube was once the frontier of the Roman Empire: you are standing somewhere that has been significant for civilisations for thousands of years. I later learned that the name Sava is also an elemental one, deriving from the Proto-Indo-European root 'sewh' meaning 'to take liquid'. The name of the water rushing around me is the same linguistic river that brings us our sip, seep, sup, sop, sap and soup.

Maga's husband, Gerhard Gesemann, would no doubt have known this – he was a Slavic language specialist, and the couple were very likely alive to such currents, for they named their daughter for a river. Rajna's name means 'paradise' in Serbian but is also the Serbian spelling for that other great European river, the Rhine, which flows through her father's native Germany. Maga's husband, who went on after their divorce to teach Slavic philology at the German University in Prague, would no doubt have enjoyed the etymology.

But Maga herself reveals strong views on the importance of naming. She begins her autobiography, *Moj Život*, with an involved description of how she came to get her family name (derived from the 'magaza' shops her ancestors owned). She also tells a story about her given names: her grandmother had wanted to name her Marija but her godfather had wanted to name her Magdalena. The priest at her christening ceremony found a compromise by writing Marija in the register but blessing the name Magdalena, the diminutive of which became the name she was best known by. I wondered how finding herself between virgin and (redeemed) whore might have influenced her dancing, with its taboo-breaking attention to the female form clad in its demure white tunic.

Now I was nearing the Captain Miša Building, an imposing Renaissance-style building constructed in 1863 by a Czech architect, appropriately near the river for its salt merchant and officially 'Danube captain' owner, Miša Anastasijević, who at one time owned 74 ships. I tried to imagine the 21-year-old Maga walking in here. Overawed? With the overconfidence of the young? A sense of mischief?

I myself was mainly overawed. The entrance hall was big and echoing, and I wasn't sure I was allowed in. However, there was nobody around to stop me so I tried to walk confidently through. Somewhere nearby, a class was in progress. Even without hearing the words distinctly or fully understanding the language properly, I could spot the rhetorical questions being asked. I imagined the echoes of Maga's own professor, Branislav Petronijević, and the comment she reports him having made on her,

'It is a pity you are so fantastical, getting carried away with acting, theatre, literature, even socialism! With a little more calmness and concentration you could develop into a solid philosophical author.'

Concentration on one thing may have been something Maga lacked: along with her other 'firsts' in so many different fields, she was also the first woman to enrol at the Law faculty – a challenge she had set for the members of her Female Students' Club. Once she had proved that registration was possible, she withdrew to continue with her philosophy degree, allowing other women to take up the places she had shown could be theirs.

Walking back through the squares of Belgrade to the Airbnb where I was staying, I saw *Politika* on sale. The newspaper was established in 1904 and is the oldest daily newspaper still in circulation in the Balkans. Only a year after it was founded, the young Maga started work there with a regular column which she used to address feminist and other avant-garde issues. One article from 1905 is titled 'Is there a profession women are not capable of?' and concludes that there is not. Bold words for 1905.

So much for Maga the student, librarian and journalist. I also needed to understand Maga the dancer. And without any forward planning I discovered that my night in Belgrade coincided with the finals of the 'Contemporary Through Time' Festival of Choreographic Miniatures in one of the auditoria of the National Theatre, with participants from Slovenia and Croatia as well as Serbia. The programme made a specific reference to Maga, noting that the festival was a continuation of her work and that 'the ideas of modern dance that Maga founded still live and evolve' through the Festival.

I don't know much about modern dance and hadn't been to a live dance performance in a quarter of a century. I certainly had no frame of reference to judge what I was going to see. But first of all it was exciting to be going to the National Theatre, the very building where Maga had gone to watch plays for free on Sundays. The architect had apparently taken the Scala in Milan as a model and the building I was seeing today had been remodelled, enlarged, war-damaged and reconstructed since then, I tried to keep

Milan in mind as I approached. Maga never did direct Shakespearean drama in this building but the event she organised to celebrate the quarter century of her dance school was held right here. As I approached tonight I saw, hanging round outside, limber-limbed youngsters in a range of warm-up positions, much as I would have seen a century before. I could feel the rush of adrenaline and butterflies – theirs and Maga's too.

The performances began on a stage with stark lighting which made dramatic shadows of the folds in the dancers' tunics, reminding me of the Brutalist lines of the Hotel Zlatibor in Užice; it threw faces and musculature into dramatic chiaroscuro. The pieces had names like 'what does the body dream?'

A girl moved puppet-like with increasing desperation, as if trying to escape her own body. A young man fought with the clothes which enveloped him, taking off layer after layer and strewing the stage with garments, each themselves in a dramatic pose – arms flung out.

The dance was alien, and alienating; beautiful but disturbing. It was a good reminder of just how shocking it must have been for Belgrade audiences to see the approaches to modern dance which Maga brought back from Berlin. Vera quotes a 1932 article in the *Nedeljne Ilustracije* 'Weekly Illustrated' magazine reflecting on Maga's first public class,

'Patriarchal … pre-war Belgrade … was stunned and defeated by the first public class of rhythmic exercises taught by Mrs Magazinović, believing the 'barefootedness' could endanger young people…

One elegant lady who had allowed her daughter to learn the… dances posed only one condition: that her daughter wore thin silk stockings … as it was rude to dance barefoot in front of an audience…The young were excited, the old saw this as an attack on "modesty" in those plastic and rhythmic exercises, and mothers feared 'catching a cold.'"

No wonder that when she opened her 'School for Declamation, Aesthetic Gymnastics and Foreign Languages' in 1910 together with a friend, Zora Prica, the Ministry advised her to 'name the school as modestly as possible so as not to scare people off.'

I don't think I am challenged by charges of immodesty but I do find the pictures I've seen of Maga dancing to be uncomfortable. In many cases they seem to be an awkward mixture of a strong, sturdy body and an assumed rather fey attitude. In one image titled 'The study of narrow motions' she holds a pose requiring both balance and steel (I felt the shudder in my thighs as I tried it). On tiptoe she tilts her upper body backwards. The bottom half of the image shows the chiselling in her calves as she pushes a toned body. But look only at the top half of the photograph and she could be a silly debutante. Her left hand goes to her chest in an 'oh my!' gesture while her right arm is crooked dramatically above her head.

Reading more about her philosophy of dance, I learned a bit more about what she was trying to achieve in showing the potential of the human body and the shapes it can form. Calling the discipline 'plastics' she defined it, according to Vera, 'as a system of gymnastic and rhythmic movements that were closely connected to breathing and psychological feeling'.

I had been using the term 'modern ballet' to refer to her work until I read her strong feelings against the term: 'Ballet depends on unnatural positions of the legs… It disfigures the human body. Modern dance rests on natural positions of the body based on the laws of motion of the human body, which have applied from ancient times to this day'.

Vera comments,

'the female body, in the way it was represented
in her own choreographies… gained new
characteristics, showing an altered, conscious
female body, which did not represent a mere
object for reproduction and male observation and
pleasure. It became a body that "thinks and speaks"
and, through dance, expresses and communicates
those female thoughts.'

And Maga wrote, 'movements of the body in dance must be liberated from the patterns of predetermined steps, jumps, turns, leans and their pre-planned order. Movements in dance must sequence and develop on their own, coming from psychological ecstasy – inspiration'.

I just wish she had had the chance to dance like some of the young women at the Festival of Choreographic Miniatures, rejoicing in muscle without having to add a skip to it. On the other hand, with the memory fresh in my mind of the exercises I'd done this morning to a YouTube video in my rented room, I saw the significance of her point when she said, 'the psyche of the person who performs body-exercises is constantly at a distance from the body which… comes down to some sort of machinery, steered by the person doing the exercise'. I was drawn to the idea of rooting my movements in psychological ecstasy rather than internet instructors.

My favourite images of Maga show her static, like the picture held at the Belgrade City Museum of her at the centre of five women. All are in the plain chiton tunics which were an iconic element in Isadora Duncan's approach to modern dance. The group is standing on a small rug which seems a health and safety hazard for a dance troupe, but on the other hand they are – famously – all barefoot so perhaps it was sensible. The group is arranged symmetrically around Maga who stands firm in the middle, chin jutting up like a defiant seer. Her arms are outstretched but not for anything as nebulous as blessing – on each arm she supports one of the other dancers who are bent backwards with arms crooked over their faces in poses of ravishment. Behind Maga two other young women hold their heads in profile, a back leg is cocked coquettishly, a hand supports a chin, like Raphael's putti. In the midst of these various transports of delight and sensibility it is Maga who holds it together – literally, with the strain in her arm muscles showing as she braces the unfurling dancers to right and left of her, but also as the point of focus of the image.

Just how successful her school was at turning out these dancers and dances it is difficult to assess. On the one hand it kept going for 25 years. On the other there's the amateur image of that description in the *Politika* article about her having to move her furniture every time the dancers come round to practise. On the one hand there's Queen Marija's attendance at performances; on the other there's the description in contemporary reviews such as that in *Balkan* in 1926 complaining about the piano accompaniments which Vera's book notes were produced by two grammar school pupils. Or the retrospective note in *Pravda* of 1938 of what had happened at the beginning of a performance: 'The lack of the audience's interest in our national reality in art was evident during Mrs Magazinović's lecture, when the bored audience entertained itself by chatting'.

The classes were free to those who could not pay – Maga noted in *Moj Život* how rich students subsidised the poor: 'for the expenses of purchasing boards, charts, paintings, I set a fee of 30 dinars per month. For the wealthier ones only. The poorer but gifted and the children of acquaintances studied for free, and it was this way during the entire 25 years.' So was this dance school just a hobby and a whimsy, or was it a serious step in Serbia's aesthetic development? Vera is sure that it was a serious enterprise. Perhaps the ambivalence about her work might be part of a wider Serbian identity crisis or crisis of confidence about dance. A 1924 article in the periodical *Vreme* asks

'Is our national dance such a treasury as are, for
example, our national poetry and national music?
Let us say that we find it to truly be a treasure
and a great wealth of diversity but that it does lag
behind the wealth of other forms of national art.
The reasons may be very simple. In times of artistic
creation our people were going through a significant
tragedy: violently taken freedom. Therefore, the

basic emotion of their creation was almost always pain. Painful national music, painful poetry, painful was even the needlework. Dance, however, being essentially cheerful and the excess strength and celebration of youth, could not develop enough under such circumstances. Instead, art forms which were better suited for pain developed.'

Perhaps Maga's dance is not putting the skip into attitudes of great emotion as I was criticising it for doing, but putting the great emotion – the pain – into what might otherwise be experienced as no more than a cheery frolic.

Certainly her classes and performances were a rallying point, or at least pet project, for many of her fellow travellers from bohemian Belgrade. Contributing musical support as a volunteer, for example, was Ksenija Atanasijević, who was just sixteen at the time. The girl later went on to study under Petronijević as Maga had done, and I learned online that in 1924 she became the first female university professor to be appointed to the Arts Faculty of the Department of Philosophy at the University of Belgrade, where she taught classics, medieval and modern philosophy and aesthetics for twelve years. During her teaching career, Ksenija was a committed feminist both in theory and practice. She was a member of the Serbian Women's League for Peace and Freedom, the Women's Movement Alliance, and editor of the first feminist journal in the country, *Ženski pokret*, 'The Women's Movement', published from 1920 to 1938.

After writing articles against anti-Semitism and National Socialism, Ksenija was arrested by the Gestapo in 1942. Then when the war ended, she was arrested again, but this time by Tito's communists on charges of war crimes. Once released, she retired in 1946 after a short stint as an employee of the National Library of Serbia.

One can only imagine the inspiration that Ksenija must have taken from Maga, and no doubt the energy that she supplied in turn to the older woman.

So Maga brought together, and possibly brought on, impressive people who were to make their mark on the country's culture in the years ahead. And Maga was sufficiently respected that she was taken on at the State Ballet School where she taught the history of dance, a subject on which she was the first to publish a book in Serbian. Her school had opened in 1910. Within two years she had ended the arrangement with Prica, who went on to hold her language classes separately. From then on Maga's school was solely for the performing arts.

Maga's energies were divided with the start of the First Balkan War in 1912, when the grammar school where she worked was transformed into a hospital and teachers were expected to work as hospital staff. In 1913 she was back in Berlin to see Gerhard but by 1914 another war had broken out. Gerhard moved to Serbia and converted to Orthodoxy so the couple could marry – in Belgrade's Cathedral – and he started working at a local school, but the marriage was to be short-lived. Gerhard left her to go as an orderly accompanying the Serbian army's withdrawal in the winter of 1915 in what is sometimes called the Great Retreat through what is today Kosovo, Montenegro and Albania, falling ill himself. Travelling by boat from Albania, he arrived in Italy and journeyed on to Switzerland.

Maga had given birth to a son who died in 1916 at less than a year old. Further loss was to come: when she went to visit Gerhard in a Swiss sanatorium he informed her that he had fallen in love with someone else and would not be coming back to Serbia.

Nevertheless, Maga apparently demanded a child by him. She stayed on in Switzerland (while there, attending a lecture by Lenin). She became pregnant with their daughter and in 1917 she gave birth in Lausanne, and returned to Belgrade with the baby. The couple finally divorced in 1923 but Gerhard did return to Belgrade and in 1939 he founded the German Institute here.

He and Maga met occasionally and it's recorded that on listening to them chatting, Gesemann's son by his second marriage, Wolfgang, commented 'why did you two divorce when you have so much to say to each other?'. Later Gerhard moved to Prague, but as a German he had to leave there, too, after the Second World War. On the journey back to Germany he lost his vast library of five thousand volumes, and a monograph on Gogol which was almost ready for publication. He died just a few years after his return to Germany, in 1948. Reading the account of their lives is almost like watching everything they had built up rewind and unravel. No doubt there's a choreographic miniature that could tell the story more powerfully than words.

Maga's other romantic relationship which I had read about had likewise been marred by loss – in her autobiography she tells the story from before her marriage of her relationship with Branko Popović, a young man also from Užice. When she was nineteen, her father called her for a 'serious conversation'.

'He told me that he had had a conversation with Branko's father and that he had told him that Branko would not be sent abroad to study painting if he did not give me up. He would stay here and would not become an artist but an engineer. I was a girl without dowry. Branko's father, as a factory owner and a businessman, only appreciated and wanted a marriage with dowry for his son.'

Vera writes of this point in Maga's life,

'her selfless decision and great emotional sacrifice enabled her first love Branko Popović to become a student of the Munich Academy and later a painter – an expressionist… one of the most prominent artistic critics of the time and one of the founders of the Association of Fine Arts in Serbia, dean of the Technical Faculty and professor of Art History at the Faculty of Architecture.'

However, even the successful Branko's life ended sadly – he was shot by the Communists without trial after the Second World War.

After she had lost a boyfriend, a son and a husband, the second half of Maga's life seems remarkable most of all for survival. Of course, the loss that I see might be more of the kind suffered by Gerhard's work on Gogol – a lacuna that is mainly documentary in nature. Throughout my reading and conversations in trying to research Maga, big gaps opened up in my patchy Serbian, often too much for Google Translate to fill. Kindly friends helped out – a member of my writer's group from some years before in Kosovo put me in touch with her professor in Belgrade who arranged for me to meet in person with Vera to whom I have so much debt for interpretation, research and commemoration of Maga's life. A colleague of my co-author's looked for a copy of *Moj Život* in Belgrade backstreets while she was on a visit to her family. I think Maga would have approved of the co-operative of women helping with the metaphorical moving back of the furniture in order to hold this dance class.

But the gaps weren't only linguistic – they were the gaps left by time, and some of those Communist bullets and the other political risks of the period. Maga's autobiography finishes in 1927. Her school closed in 1935.

In 1936 she did found a Students Folk Group for traditional dances, to which she gave a particular spin. Vera notes of her treatment of the story of the fourteenth century Battle of Kosovo, for example, that although 'the whole Kosovo heroic myth was based on a man, even the epic poem named after a female character, The Kosovo Maiden, represented the story of the honourable death of knights i.e. the male population.'

Maga nevertheless staged her dances from the point of view of the mothers of significant characters.

She took her Folk Group to Hitler's Germany which might be another reason for her absence in the social and cultural life of post-war, Communist Belgrade. After that, apart from a tantalising reference to her in Nice in 1938 (I imagine her on the seafront, face lifted to the sun), I know nothing else about her until her death in 1968 – that year when Europe's students rose up, two generations after her Female Students' Club, and America saw the feminist protest against the 'degrading Mindless-Boob-Girlie Symbol' of the Miss America pageant. Maga's work was far from done, but it seemed her ideas on where power should be located were gaining ground.

And what has she left us? A slew of articles from her time on *Politika*, her books on the history of dance, and her autobiography; a street name in the Serbian capital, and a mural in her hometown. A Serbian postage stamp was also issued to commemorate her in 2019, and there's a Serbian ballet studio named for her, perhaps unaware of her feelings about classical ballet.

But of course she's left us more than that – in the inspiration she gave, and continues to give, and the doors she opened not only for herself, but to let others in after her – whether those who enrolled in the Law faculty after her example, or women inspired by her newspaper column or the dancers in her classes which offered a forum where women could discover their power and ownership over their bodies. Walking past the City Museum on my journey out of Belgrade, I wondered whether that was why their photograph of her surrounded by four other dancing women made such an impression on me. Not just for her strength and place at the heart of the energies of a dance, but because her arms are outstretched not in pleading, but in support: her muscles enabling the swooning backbends of the women dancing around her, and eventually off and away from her.

* We are grateful to Ivana Brakočević and Stevan Mrdjenović for all the translations which appear here taken from the English version of Vera Obradović Ljubinković's book.

Chapter 5

For whom the streets have no name: Margaret Hasluck and the unwritten law in Albania

The guest must call out before coming into the house; the host must come out and take the guest's gun. It must be hung on a hook and the guest accompanied to the fireplace. The guest must be offered 'bread, salt and your heart' at any hour of day or night.

The guest should be the first to drink coffee but the host the first to drink the raki brandy. If the host dares to take a bite of food before the guest, he is fined 500 *grosh*.

These, and many other minute stipulations come from one of the Albanians' most important texts, the Kanun. It's a set of rules passed down in an oral tradition which goes back certainly to the Middle Ages, and perhaps beyond (some commentators have found links within it to the Homeric code of hospitality).

The book's chapter on hosting guests (tellingly, within the section on 'honour') sets out the rules for this element of human interaction as fastidiously as are the details of every other area of life (and death) across this extraordinary work.

To give some context, and an idea of the frame of reference of the Kanun, the 500 *grosh* fine for tucking into your food before your visitor does is the same fine as for stealing a goat or a beehive; the same price you're expected to pay to cover new shoes for a person you appoint to do the reconciliation of your family with someone you're in blood feud with; two thirds of the fine set for shooting someone in the leg; sufficient to cover the fines payable for swearing five times in church; it's enough to buy ten good baking trays at the price set by the Kanun, and is 100 times the tip owing to the woman who dresses a bride on her wedding day.

Baffled? Intrigued? Margaret Hasluck was, and in 1927 – as a 42-year-old widow – this determined Scot set off to Albania to find out more about the society ruled by such ancient laws. She ended up staying twelve years, working her way into the heart of the country; living in the town of Elbasan, a town about as plumb centre in the middle of Albania as you can get. She became a familiar figure in the town, known simply as 'Englezka' – The Englishwoman.

Her book, *The Unwritten Law in Albania*, was published posthumously in 1954. With named examples of its application among the people she had met in communities around Albania, the medieval law is brought to life. Her book was never going to be a best-seller, and yet one feels that any one of the case histories that are shared could be the basis for a soap opera or thriller. And despite the fact that this 'new information of great interest for the ethnologist ... with great clarity and sympathy' is also described in a contemporary review as resembling 'clinical reports without interpretation,' I somehow found I couldn't stop reading.

'When a house dog attacked a stranger, the law considered three positions: a) when the dog only threatened to bite, b) when it succeeded in biting and c) when it killed. In all three positions there was discrimination between attack by day and attack by night… If during the daytime a house dog succeeded in biting a stranger, its master must indemnify the stranger…. He must keep the wounded man in his house free of charge until he recovered, pay any doctor's bills that might be incurred and pay the wounded man what he would have earned if well.'

'If a shooting dog put up a hare, only its master had the right to take the hare. It might be that the chase was long and that the hare was shot by a stranger before the dog's master caught it up. In that case, the latter demanded the hare and offered the stranger a fresh cartridge in return for the one he had just expended, If the offer was refused, a blood feud started.'

'A man could not, without the elders' consent, close an old road that, having been used by his fellow-travellers, bridal parties and funeral processions, was public property. … If he had ploughed it up, so that its line was uncertain, they sought out an old trustworthy man and made him show them under oath and in the presence of witnesses where it had been. Then the offender was ordered to open it again, … and, by way of a penalty, to give a meal and small fee to the old man and the witnesses. If he shut it up once more, he was liable to be shot.'

It's the intriguing mix of old courtesy – opening your home to the injured, offering a fellow hunter a fresh cartridge, serving a meal for a trustworthy old man – followed by the brutality of that final sentence which makes the book so strangely compelling.

Among other things, Hasluck's work covers the precedents and principles of ploughing, water rights, and footpath widths. In places it reads like the minutes of a parish council meeting. And of course it was ironic to produce a written account of these laws; if Hasluck had been Albanian she would have perhaps shared her findings instead in a 'pleqnar' – one of the meetings convened in the villages for resolution of issues via debate. The elders would sit cross-legged on sheepskin and lumpily stuffed palliasses, ranged round the edges (a man's closeness to the hearth indicating his seniority) of an 'oda', a council and hospitality room on the top floor of one of the most significant stone houses in the neighbourhood.

In fact, if she had been Albanian, she wouldn't have had the opportunity to take part in such a meeting. Even the coffee was served to the *pleqnar* not by women but by adolescent boys. Oestrogen had no place in an oda.

But the laws were not the only unwritten traditions that Hasluck wrote down. Women may not have been allowed to loll against the *odas'* cushions, but you can be sure they had their own ways of knowing, passing down, and nicely judging behaviour in relation to social rules. The men's rules certainly didn't stop Hasluck's work as a keen folklorist. During her time living in Albania she'd collected stories, one of which, I was told, was narrated to her by an Elbasan schoolboy, Mahir Domi. Domi was later to become a distinguished scholar of Albanian customs and culture and one day, while researching Hasluck's story, I even found myself walking down a street named for him in Kosovo's capital, Prishtina.

Domi's schoolboy days were before the Second World War and he had now died, but his daughter lived in Tirana where she worked as Deputy Director of the National Library. If I couldn't meet Margaret Hasluck, I could follow the oral tradition of talking to a woman who'd talked to her father who'd narrated a story to Hasluck.

How to make contact with this woman, Etleva? My friend Dorina, who is from Elbasan, had offered to try to find Etleva's number. She thought her mother would have it so, while Dorina and I had a drink together, she called her mum. There was no answer so she said that since her mother was bad at remembering to take her phone with her, she'd call her mother's friend who was probably with her. She called this friend. No, she wasn't with Dorina's mother but could she help at all? Dorina explained what we wanted. Oh yes, the friend was at that minute drinking coffee with someone from the Domi family.

'Here's the number,' said Dorina.

Margaret Hasluck would have told me that in Albania, oral traditions are always the most reliable sources of information.

Etleva said that I could 'come any time' to meet her at the National Library but I fixed a time all the same. I set off for the meeting promptly, but when I got to the city's main square, on the eastern side of which lay the library, I discovered the enormous works which lay between me and my meeting.

As the main space in the main city in the country, the area of what is now known as Skanderbeg Square has always been an index to power. It's named for the Albanian national hero of the fifteenth century, and it used to be dominated by a sturdy metal statue of the country's dictator, Enver Hoxha. It had been to Hoxha that Hasluck had written to plead for the life of her good friend (Hoxha alleged that the man was her lover), Lef Nosi when he was on trial in 1946. The letter's pleading had fallen on tin-deaf ears and after a trial held in what the British Military Mission at the time described as a 'squalid' Tirana cinema, Lef was executed in February 1946.

Almost 45 years to the day after Lef's execution, the massive bulk of the Enver Hoxha statue was pulled down by a crowd of protestors filling this square with pent-up student frustration. Once again, it was in this public space that you could read the dynamics of power, traced and smashed against the stones.

And now there was a new mayor in town and his vision was again being spelt out here. In his case, literally. A creative refurb of the square included a hopscotch made from stones sourced from around Albania (an informational panel told you from exactly where), on which were engraved the Albanian words for 'better', 'much', 'together', 'we are', 'we become', 'when', 'you', 'I'.

The bid for democracy could not be clearer. Here's your public space; you write the poem. It's your own body's motion that creates a verse…

Would Margaret and Lef have ever believed this could be possible?

But it turns out that even the best democracy needs a high fence around it, and while the transformation of Skanderbeg Square was underway – while Albania's first ecological recycled asphalt was being laid, and the seeds and saplings planted for rewilding of one corner and all the other free verse was being written – the area was out of bounds.

I caught a snatch of laughter from the vast concrete pyramid across the boulevard, built for Enver Hoxha's tomb.

To get to my meeting at the National Library with Etleva Domi to talk about Margaret Hasluck I had to find a way round this blocked-off square. I could see the entrance of the library through the modular railings that towered over head-height, but to take the route around the fencing would add about a kilometre to my journey. I would be late.

A gap had been left in the railings where the weighted rubber socket blocks hadn't been placed quite flush together. One of the many signs announcing the impossibility of crossing the square hung just beside the gap. I approached it.

I had made my way halfway across the square when a man in a hi-vi jacket saw me and wagged his finger.

'Just to the National Library,' I said, continuing my trajectory, though more slowly now.

I was in my poncho and I had my Nikon hung round my neck. I couldn't have looked more foreign.

There was a silence. It lasted for the time that it would take to say, 'The Albanian's home belongs to God and the guest'.

The length of time it would take to carefully enunciate 'he was liable to be shot.'

Hi-vi guy's superior called out to him,

'Let her pass.' There are rules, and then there are guests in your country. There is the unwritten law.

Wriggling through the space left in the fence at the other end of the work site, I got to the library just on time.

At Etleva's office it was suggested that while she finished a meeting, I could register as a library reader. I'd brought my passport and two photographs with me for just such an eventuality and I handed them to the librarian.

'Now please read this,' she said, 'and tell me if there's anything you don't understand'. A laminated notice stood on her desk and I expected to have to read something like the promise I'd made at the Bodleian library I'd made as an Oxford undergraduate, 'not to kindle flame'.

'From 5 February,' the notice said, 'we will have restricted services'. It went on to list the reduced facilities that would be available though it all seemed quite reasonable – 24 hours from a request being filed to your book being available.

I was issued with a card and the helpful librarian showed me how to fill in the request slip. I waited for Etleva at one of the few spare desks and looked around. I calculated that there were 80 seats here and the majority were full, with almost twice as many women as men studying. It was a contented, purposeful atmosphere.

Soon there was the sound of the heels of a determined woman walking briskly into the reading room, and a voice introduced herself to me as Etleva. She ushered me into her office and I explained why I was here – wanting to talk to someone who had talked to someone who had talked to Margaret Hasluck.

As she settled me into the office, walled with folders and stacks of encyclopaedias, she explained,

'My father didn't actually talk to Margaret Hasluck, I'm afraid. He was a schoolboy when she asked the class not to tell her but to write down the traditional stories they knew. I know that's not what you want to hear, but I was keen to meet you so that's why I invited you to visit.' The Albanian love of guests.

I tried not to let my disappointment show, and asked her more about the incident. She said that her father would have been 13 years old. The story he wrote down was called 'The Wild Horses' and was chosen for publication in Hasluck's book *Këndime Englisht-Shqip or Albanian-English reader: sixteen Albanian folk-stories collected and translated, with two grammars and vocabularies*, which came out in 1932. Etleva said that he had seen this as his first publication and the start of his interest in philology.

After we'd talked some more, she showed me out and offered any help she could give for my research, 'You can use the Paolo Petta room,' she said as she escorted me into the reading room. She spoke in a tone just like the hi-vi guy's boss outside, and I was taken past the rows of reading desks where I'd sat and waited.

'You can be quiet here,' she promised, 'And there's Wi-Fi.' It sounded like an executive lounge at an airport and I wondered whether there might be free croissants too.

'And we will bring you the book you ordered right away.'

But I knew the (written) rules – I had been watched reading them, had had to confirm that I understood them… It should take 24 hours for my book to arrive. And yet *Per çdo mik duhet buka si han vetë*. The Albanian word 'buka' didn't actually mean 'book' – though I'd privately enjoyed the pun of this essential of life. What the Kanun specified was that your guest should have the same *food* as you yourself were consuming. But the librarians seemed to be taking the principle into an unstinting nourishing of my mind.

I sat in the cosy room, and settled into the book I'd ordered up. It was *Elbasan Folktales* by Astrit Bishqemi. In the introduction he says he spoke to a retired teacher who told him how the Englezka occasionally went to their school and into class to speak to the pupils. Her other recollection of Hasluck was of what she did with meat she bought – boiling up the innards up to drink as stock, but distributing the flesh to the poor.

The book includes the 'Wild Horses' story which Etleva's father had retold to Hasluck. It's a strange dark tale like an amalgam of many others; like the dream you might have after a big supper of cheese. There are three brothers, four horses, magical suits which are used for a wedding at the palace, a king who wants to get married to his daughter, a black ram and a white, a devil who eats a person every day – a Freudian fantasy like Cinderella meets *Joseph and the Technicolour Dreamcoat* meets Electra.

The hero is of course the youngest brother, whose name is what I learned to be a traditional name for this folklore character. Qeros means 'ringworm' and little Ringworm first of all captures the wild horses without the advantage of the guns that his brothers had tried to use, but with cunning and bravery alone. He's then abandoned by his brothers and in revenge drags them and their wives naked behind a horse though at the end 'they crowned him king and with his bride and his mother they ruled and lived happily together'.

The book had last been requested by a reader five years before. I could read his name on the record on the back. My name was written there too. No surname, just 'Elizabeth'. It made me feel like Englezka.

Thanks to the library's hospitality, I was also able to read Hasluck's original *Albanian-English Reader*. It's dedicated to Lef Nosi, the friend whose life Hasluck had unsuccessfully pleaded for. I knew that Edith Durham, the British traveller, anthropologist, humanitarian and writer who had been the subject of my second book had considered Nosi 'the only Albanian who understood the value of folklore'. A former headmaster, he had been one of the signatories of Albania's Declaration of Independence in 1912 and had then served as Minister of Economy and been a member of the Albanian delegation to the Paris Peace Conference in 1919. By the time Hasluck met him, he had retired from politics and dedicated himself to scholarship.

Hasluck later wrote,

'Had we been younger when we met – and richer – we would have married... He had no money and I

… had only what I put into the house. What we had without marriage was very wonderful – an almost perfect intellectual fit and complete similarity of ideals.'

It was to Nosi's care that Hasluck left both her house and her 3,000-book library when she was expelled from Albania in 1939 on charges of espionage. She never returned to Albania – her final offering to the country was to give a rose to a general she knew who was due to visit, asking him to leave it on Nosi's grave.

She also honoured the memory of that library left behind. When she died (of leukaemia) in 1948, part of her bequest to the University of Oxford was found to be allocated 'to establish a fund known as the Lef Nosi of Elbasan, Albania, Memorial Fund'. She required the university to 'apply it in the first instance to the purchase of books on Albania in accordance with the frontiers in 1939, and … insert in each book so bought a book-plate with the inscription "Bequest by Margaret Hasluck in grateful memory of Lef Nosi of Elbasan, Albania."'

I liked the idea that this book dedicated to Lef Nosi which I was reading in a building just off Skanderbeg Square had sisters and brothers in the reading rooms of the English town where I'd sworn not to kindle flame.

Hasluck's vision for this *Albanian-English reader* was cute – to share traditional tales in English and Albanian and use them as the basis for learners to assimilate the language. It might have been better if the stories weren't so chaotic (a reader of 'Wild Horses' could be forgiven for assuming some mistranslation) but also perhaps if the narratives were closer to the vocabulary needed for daily life. A sample of the glossary gives a glimpse of the language you could master this way – 'boar, board, body, boiler, bolster, bone, bore, bosom, both, bottom.'

What might have been a purely pedagogical quibble when the book came out in 1932 had, by 1942, become a matter of life and death. It was at this point that Hasluck was taken on by the British government as Adviser on Albanian Affairs to brief Special Operations Executive (SOE) agents being dropped into Albania.

It wasn't the first time that Hasluck had done 'special' work – she had had a minor role during the First World War with British intelligence in Athens, and boasted of having smuggled letters between Athens and London in her garters. Now she was supporting agents whose aim was to boost local attempts to fight the Germans. They were also tasked with gathering intelligence about the rival factions of the Communists and the Balli Kombëtar 'National Front' and which of them the British government should back.

It is not clear that Hasluck's quirky, folklore-based methods were quite what was needed to prepare these men for parachuting into enemy territory.

Bought, bow, bowl, box, boy, bramble, brave.

The story of Kocamici, written by Lef Nosi and included in her Reader, is of a mouse that fell into a pot. Hasluck made her 'boys' learn some lines by heart. Anthony Quayle (yes, that Anthony Quayle – of *The Guns of Navarone*, *Lawrence of Arabia* and *The Eagle has Landed*, among many other film and stage appearances) reports defusing 'a heated meeting between rival guerrillas when, just as a revolver was being loosened in its holster,' he broke in suddenly with a line from Kocamici. Another of the operatives used the well-rehearsed Kocamici lines as a greeting to the man in goatskin and bandolier who came to meet him when his parachute landed. It's great stuff for situation comedy, but less impressive as the basis of a briefing for military intelligence.

Hasluck's superiors in SOE certainly had their reservations about her. 'The usual waffle,' wrote Major Peter Boughey, of SOE's Balkan and Middle East desk, across one of Hasluck's letters in November 1943. By 1944 she had resigned.

The young men recruited to the SOE for missions in Albania mention Hasluck with a mixture of affection and exasperation. In his book, *Albanian Assignment*, David Smiley says she reminded him of an old-fashioned English nanny. Peter Kemp's description of her in his book, *No Colours or Crest* is of 'a grey, birdlike woman who made up in energy and determination what she lacked in patience… when we were in the field we would often receive signals from her directing our attention to some beauty spot nearby where we could enjoy a picnic.' Bailey reports SOE officer Reginald Hibbert saying of her 'it was a bit like having Enid Blyton in charge.'

One wonders whether these men were just racking their brains for comparators. Perhaps there were not many women other than nannies and writers of children's stories who had held positions of authority in their lives? Roderick Bailey, in his book *The Wildest Province: SOE in the land of the eagle* describes how Hugh Munro, 'a Gordon Highlander and fellow Scot, who "got on famously" with Hasluck before leaving for Albania in 1944 ... "got one hell of a bollocking off her once for barging into her room without knocking"' which seems fair enough to me.

Certainly, her men's affection or loyalty to her was real – both Quayle and another SOE operative, Billy McLean, made anonymous payments into her bank account later when they heard she was in financial difficulty. And the nation was also grateful – 1944 Hasluck was offered an MBE for her work as the government's Adviser on Albanian Affairs though she turned the award down.

Pictures of her survive, though they don't match well with some of the reminiscences of those who knew her or accounts by those who've interviewed them. David Smiley mentions her 'pink complexion with bright blue eyes' and 'greying hair swept back into a bun' while Bailey describes her arriving in Istanbul – where she was tasked with contacting Turkey's Albanian community to find volunteers prepared to work for the British – 'under an assumed name and with dyed hair,' (what is this obsession with what the woman's hair was like?). Despite the suggestions of frailty in many of these descriptions, she herself relates how she was taken for a man – 'tall, dressed in overcoat and a soldier's fustanella.'

I was able to hear another opinion of Hasluck from David Shankland, the Director of the Royal Anthropological Institute, who invited me to give a presentation there about my work on Edith Durham – the Institute's former Vice President. After the lecture I was invited to tea and the subject of Hasluck came up. Despite their common interest and activities over a similar period, I could find little evidence of common ground between these two Albanophile women – the only point of contact I'd seen being some carping notes from Durham scribbled on an article by Hasluck which had been sent to her for review. There was no doubt professional rivalry and Bailey compares the two to Durham's discredit, saying of Hasluck that 'in methodology and commitment she far outpassed Edith Durham who, though better known, never learnt the language and spent just a fraction of Hasluck's sixteen years in the country.'

Shankland has edited three volumes on the life of Margaret's husband, Frederick William Hasluck, who died of TB in 1920, before any of her adventures in Albania began. David's view of the poor press Margaret received was that she could seem to others to be arrogant, which upset them. His casual comments which I gleaned between our biscuit crumbs in Fitzrovia are backed up by some documentary references which suggest that it was in part because of Margaret that Frederick's work as Assistant Director of the British School in Athens was cut short. An incoming director, Wace, who harboured animosity towards Margaret, requested that her husband was sacked.

I was inclined to think this a petty ex-pat drama but David reminded me,

> 'it was hardly petty. Her husband lost his position, was excluded from the British School at Athens and died partly because of the conditions he had thereby to live in: Wace triumphed by staying as Director, obtained exemption from war service, and gained a

professorship in Cambridge. It was the opposite of petty, but gravely serious: one man died, the other flourished. Ruthless would be closer to the mark.'

The characters in the tragedy are represented in scarcely-disguised form in Olivia Manning's *Fortunes of War*, based on her own experiences in Athens in the same years around the outbreak of the First World War. A vignette of the character Mrs Brett leaves a vivid impression of what Hasluck might have been like. Here she is narrating her experience with a drunk Australian,

> "'Of course I know how to deal with men in that state," Mrs Brett said, "I've had experience of all sorts, and it pays to be agreeable. Talk to them, get them interested; so I said, 'Sit down, there's a good fellow, and I'll order you some tea.'" The Australian had seated himself "like a lamb" but unfortunately knocked over a chair... "We had a nice long chat and he showed me all the photographs in his wallet – Mum and Dad and Sis and so on... I said 'Don't be alarmed.... I understand men: this poor boy's missing his mother,' 'You're right, mem,' said my Australian. 'I never had a mom like the other fellas.' 'Now, now,' I said, 'What about that snapshot you just showed me?' 'That's the old man's second wife,' he said. 'And a right cow she is.' What a fascinating language! At last I said, nicely but firmly, 'I have to go now. You come tomorrow and have tea at my flat and you can tell me all your troubles.'"

'Nice but firm' – I mused that these described just some of the qualities that would be needed by a lone foreign woman in a small town, venturing out to take down notes of local disputes over dogs or rights of way, and to distribute food parcels and speak to local children about their fairy tales. I still couldn't quite imagine Hasluck's life in Albania. Bailey describes how

> 'she journeyed all over the country, alone, in all weathers and by all modes of transport, spending whole seasons in the mountains. Collecting folktales and songs was a constant passion but her extensive notes and data covered a wide variety of topics: from local dialects, coinage and customs, to witches, blood feuds and botany. She sent dozens of artefacts to Aberdeen's Marischal Museum.'

I headed to the Albanian town of Elbasan which had been her base, to see what trace of Hasluck I could find there. My route was along a new road, proudly – not to say extravagantly – built just recently. In fact, as with Skanderbeg Square in Tirana, this was another piece of public highway whose full length I was not permitted to travel. In this case it was because some of it was blocked by protests against the tolls that had been set up to pay for its extravagance.

Though the road might be new, the route was an ancient one – Elbasan lay on the Via Egnatia which linked Rome to Constantinople. That road, named for the Governor of Macedonia, Gnaeus Egnatius, who began the road's construction, started at the port of Durrës and was what the Apostle Paul journeyed along.

Not much of that former glory remained. It was a late winter day and I felt like I was travelling through a landscape of leftovers. The conical haystacks supported on their central sticks had been munched through like pears nibbled to the core. There were still ruddy persimmons hanging in the trees but they seemed like forgotten Christmas decorations. Bunkers bulging in the fields below were abandoned remains too – the almost indestructible remnants of Enver Hoxha's paranoia. The vicious suspicion which had forced Hasluck out of the country and sentenced Lef Nosi to death had created these pillboxes in which each family could defend themselves against the enemies Hoxha had imagined massing on the borders. Hoxha and his statue might be gone, but some of his creations were yet to be fully dismantled.

In Elbasan I walked down the main street, named for Lef Nosi, to a meeting set up for me at the university with Rudolf Deliana. He was born in 1931 so was now in his eighties, and had memories of seeing Hasluck when he was a child. As we sat in a university office, he reminisced about passing her house with its 'strange' low wall with iron railings above it. Albanian houses are typically completely walled off from the road so this freakish transparency left an impression. 'We'd look over the wall at the flowers.' He remembered the garden as 'beautiful', and that she had employed a gardener.

He commented, 'she had lovely curtains and big windows – it was an ordinary house for England but for us it was extraordinary.'

Rudolf mentioned, too, how she had loved what I heard as 'masa'. This fitted with the stern picture given by her military contacts – a woman who loved 'taking measures'. I followed up,

'What kind of *masa*?' but Rudolf saw my misunderstanding. Not *masa* but *maca*.

'Miaow, miaow,' he mimicked with a crinkled smile. It was cats that Hasluck had loved! 'Oh yes,' he said. 'Everyone had wondered at how she treated those cats – they had a bed and she even bought them meat.'

Gently, I probed further about public opinion – what had people thought about her attempts to save Lef Nosi – her letter to Enver Hoxha pleading for his life.

'People appreciated it,' he said. 'In silence.'

It would, no doubt, have been reckless to be vocal.

My meeting with Rudolf had been arranged by Teuta Toska, a professor at the university with a professional interest in Hasluck. We discussed Hasluck's legacy – her writing and the memories she'd left behind. 'Is there a plaque on her house?' I asked, and Teuta looked uncomfortable.

'There used to be, but it's not there anymore.'

'So there's no commemoration of her in Elbasan at all?' I asked.

'I did go to the municipality,' said Teuta, 'and asked whether she could be commemorated in a road name.' It was a good point, and I thought about Skanderbeg, Gnaeus Egnatius, Lef Nosi, Mahir Domi... What was it that they had had which Margaret Hasluck had not?

Teuta said she had met with the head of the terrifying-sounding municipal Committee for Evaluating Public Figures who confirmed that a request for a road named for Hasluck had been made. But it was just that… no road had actually been given that name. The unwritten law.

'But you can still see the house where Hasluck lived,' she offered. This was apparently now Public Kindergarten No. 17 (Albanian authorities don't mess around with Little Nippers, Busy Bees and Nutkins for their pre-school names) and she knew the part of town where we could find it, though not the exact address.

On the way, we stopped at Nosi's house, now a charity's headquarters, but still an elegant building which retained some of the features that would have been familiar to him seventy years ago. There was beautiful carving over the doorways and a view over pantiled roofs – now over a mosque in one direction and a church in another – to the mountains beyond.

But it was Hasluck's home we'd really come to see and we continued through the neighbourhood to Kindergarten No. 17. Teuta stopped to speak to a woman perhaps in her sixties, who was passing. Could she tell us the way to the kindergarten?

'Kindergarten number 17? Oh yes, it's in the Englezka's house,' the woman said.

When we reached it, we found a low villa, still with an attractive garden – and a man working to keep it so, just as it had in Englezka's time. The garden walls were muralled with rainbows and cheery pictures – including, I noticed with pleasure – one of a ginger cat. But for all the hope for the future that education gives, it wasn't the upbeat tone of the activities in Kindergarten No. 17 that inspired me.

It was the co-ordinates we'd been given by that ordinary woman of Elbasan in order to find it. Hasluck was remembered! The loyalty to her memory by a passer-by in an Albanian side street was at last a tribute I knew she would have valued. So much of her life had seemed to be loss and rejection – rejection for her and her husband from the British School of Athens, a widowhood that began at age 35, expulsion from Albania, the resignation from her work as Adviser on Albanian Affairs, the MBE she turned down, Nosi's execution, even the commemorative plaque now missing from the wall of her old house and the road that had never been named for her. But here in the country she'd loved, even seventy years after her death, there were people who'd never met her who used her and her home as a reference point in conversation. The power of unwritten law.

Chapter 6

Shote Galica
and the women of Kosovo

A nation needs a legend. A legend takes an individual story and makes it general. Instead of the jungle of a nation's histories, it's much easier to find ourselves in one story, one character.

A war of hate needs a story of love.

Kosovo has been a unit of something bigger, ruled by someone else, for much longer than it has been a country. It was, at different times, part of provinces of the Roman, Bulgarian, Serbian and Ottoman Empires. It gained its current borders as a province of Yugoslavia, and declared independence within them in 2008.

Kosovo has proved more resilient as an idea than as a set of borders. Inconveniently, it has been conflicting ideas. For Serbs, the folk memory of significant reversals in their mediaeval history makes Kosovo, in a strange predisposition to melancholy, the touchstone of their nationhood. For Albanians, the vast majority of Kosovo's population from before the twentieth century, and denied full democratic rights there throughout it, Kosovo has been an open wound of oppression, and a dream of liberty.

In a land of disputed histories – without the identity that comes from a coherent entity organising itself, no history of statehood so no statesmen, no tradition of education to produce people to make, write and read history – role models are hard to find.

In the cafes, when conversation turns to the women of Kosovo's history, everyone says: please, don't make it about Shote Galica.

$$\sim$$

Shote Galica, bandit heroine of Kosovo, had enough to fight against.

She was born in 1895, when Kosovo was still a district of the Ottoman Empire. She was raised in two systems of oppression: as a subject of the Ottomans, abandoned or abused according to the distant whim of Istanbul; and as a woman in a traditional society still governed by a mediaeval folk law, in which 'woman is a sack for carrying things', a father or husband's property to be traded. When she took up with Azem Galica in 1915, Kosovo had been shared out as part of the booty of the Balkan wars, and then overrun by the Bulgarians (another heroic Serb defeat) and Austro-Hungarians during the First World War.

Shote and Azem were fighting for much of their ten years together. Kosovo's village warriors resisted the Serbs who came marauding during the Balkan wars, and then they resisted the Bulgarians and Austrians who defeated and displaced the Serbs a couple of years later. Kosovo always seems to be the cockpit for bigger external players fighting a bigger external battle: Ottomans versus Hungarians et al. in the fourteenth and fifteenth centuries;

Serbs versus, variously, Ottomans, Bulgarians, Germans and indeed NATO in the twentieth; today the EU, Russia and (still) Turkey vie for influence. The people of Kosovo seem generally to have been fighting to be left alone, rather than for any greater strategy. At the end of the First World War, the Serbs were back again and Kosovo was part of the Kingdom of Serbs, Croats and Slovenes. In sporadic risings and persistent banditry during the early 1920s, thousands of ethnic Albanian 'kaçaks' (from the Turkish word for outlaw) resisted the new regime in Kosovo and neighbouring provinces, supported by a Committee for the National Defence of Kosovo that had been formed by Kosovo exiles in Albania. Azem Galica, with Shote beside him, was prominent among them.

There is one photo of them together, in matching outfits of a simple dark version of highland dress, with the white felt hat traditional among the Albanians, and the superabundance of weapons likewise. Husband and wife have pistols tucked into their waist sashes, and each holds a rifle. He sits, looking uncomfortable and even alarmed by the camera, eyes wide over his finely waxed moustache. She stands beside him, a hand pressing on his shoulder. Hers is a strong pose – femininity sacrificed to the obligation of war – and she glowers indifferent at the viewer.

Azem was mortally wounded in conflict in 1924. The story goes that he asked to be tended and then buried in a cave, so that the Serbs would not find him. A century later, a hand-painted sign on the main road west from Prishtina claimed dubiously to identify the cave. The story further goes that Shote took over leadership of his band, and continued to fight the Serbs for two more years. In another tale, she took part in the capture or assassination of a Serbian official in Mitrovica. The effort to carve out an autonomous space in Kosovo overlapped with the violent politics of 1920s Albania, always a hinterland of refuge and supply for ethnic Albanian efforts in Kosovo; the highland fighters from Kosovo and the north tended to resist the power grab by the man who would become King Zog. Their instinct for an isolated local freedom would flicker again, with similar futility, against the communists at the end of the Second World War. After another round of fighting in Kosovo, having lost much of her family to war and suffering from her accumulated wounds, Shote Galica withdrew to Albania for the last time. The paralysed fingers of her right hand had to be amputated; she was obliged to sell her husband's horse – in the story, an ultimate sacrifice. She died in Albania in 1927, aged 32.

On such a fragmentary record, it's easier to base a legend than an essay. It is hard to grasp the reality of Kosovo in the early twentieth century – harder to grasp the daily lives of its people, and particularly its women – when the few accounts that exist focus entirely on conflict. Shote Galica is alleged to have said that 'life without knowledge is like a war without weapons'; the analogy is appropriately martial, but it seems an unlikely – or at best a plaintive – remark from a woman whom society and circumstances deprived of education.

$\sim$

Kosovo was the no-man's land of Woodrow Wilson's century of self-determination. At the Conference of London in 1913 the Great Powers defined a new Albania but – as a compromise between their own competing concerns in the Balkans – left predominantly Albanian Kosovo out of it. Swallowed by the First World War, and almost forgotten in the Versailles carve-up, Albania was rescued from the debris by the American President. But Kosovo – along with ethnic Albanian populations in Greece, Montenegro and today's Macedonia – was still outside, and absorbed into what became Yugoslavia. The Second World War brought another heroic Serb defeat, and another foreign occupation of Kosovo (Germans, Bulgarians, and Italians); and then another Serb return, and a new regime – this time Tito's communists. Under Tito, Kosovo secured autonomy within Yugoslavia, but after his death the rise of Slobodan Milošević and the country's civil war saw Kosovo's autonomy suppressed and Kosovo's Albanians excluded from public employment and education, and increasingly brutalised. At least once in each generation – the twenties, the forties, the late sixties, the eighties and nineties – they have known oppression, resistance, instability and constitutional uncertainty. By the mid-1990s, with Kosovo again left out of an international peace settlement of the Balkans, oppression had again prompted armed resistance in the villages.

Among the highest profile heroes of the Kosovo Liberation Army in the late nineties were Fehmi Lladrovci and his wife Xhevë Krasniqi Lladrovci. He was born perhaps ten miles from Azem Galica's birthplace and just a mile or so from where Shote is said to have caught the Serbian commander, in the Drenica valley which has been central to resistance in Kosovo. Xhevë was the daughter of a political activist renowned for having found the bones of

Azem Galica. They led an armed band in the early phase of the insurgency against Milošević's forces, when it was trying to hold isolated bits of rural Kosovo and carrying out sporadic guerrilla attacks. On the 22nd of September 1998, resisting a regime offensive, their armed group became increasingly beleaguered and eventually surrounded. Fehmi Lladrovci was mortally wounded, and ordered those left with him to slip away. His wife refused. Beside her husband's body, Xhevë Krasniqi Lladrovci fought on until she too was killed. A war of hate needs a story of love.

In his book on Azem and the Drenica resistance, Ibrahim Çitaku describes the reaction of a group of listeners to Azem and Shote recounting their battle experiences: 'Many of them noted in particular her seriousness, modesty and sincerity'; camp-fire heroine she might be, but never inappropriate. In the book's description of Azem and co. defending a house from attack – with a resonant prefiguring of the fatal assault on liberation hero Adem Jashari and his family at their home in Prekaz in 1998 – there's an implicit contrast between Shote, shooting cheerfully and competitively at the attackers, and the more conventional womanly service provided by Azem's mother Sherife, supplying the fighters with ammunition. Writing on the ninetieth anniversary of her death, Mehmet Bislimi addressed Shote Galica's maternal qualities:

> 'As a mother, Shote did not have the chance to enjoy the caresses of her son, who died very soon after birth in the mountainous conditions. Yet she did

not feel indifferent to those instincts; rather she took with her the children of friends who had died for Kosovo's freedom. Not for one moment would she leave them alone, becoming a second mother to them right to the very end of her own life.'

Apparently Shote's warrior lifestyle might make us worry that she was somehow deficient or deprived of crucial elements of womanliness. Apparently we can be reassured. Apparently this is important.

In the highland culture of the Albanians, a perceived need to regulate and police the role and even concept of womanhood has led to a distinctive phenomenon: the 'sworn virgins' – the 'women who become men' of the title of Antonia Young's pioneering study – a number of whom were still going strong well into the twenty-first century and who have tended every few years to crop up as an ethnological curiosity feature in some western European magazine.

In simple terms, the phenomenon is the answer to what happens in an isolated and patriarchal society, where both property and gender roles are tightly regulated by traditional law codes, when a male head of household dies leaving no male successor. In the Albanian highlands, where a 'village' is a widely- and sparsely-scattered collection of semi-fortified family houses, the male head of family has a significant and quasi-legal role as both the ultimate arbiter of all that happens within the family, and the family's representative within the wider community. It is inconceivable for a distinct family to exist without one. Accordingly, in extremis a woman from the family has to 'become' a man: both in terms of outward tokens (clothing, custody and use of the family rifle, openly smoking) and of status within home and community. Little is ever said about any other instincts or inclinations when a woman puts on the pants, especially when there's more than one sister and it's not necessarily the eldest. But it is generally presented as a sacrifice: a regrettable abandonment of an individual identification as a woman, and thus of the satisfactions and obligations of womanhood, in the interests of communal stability maintained through and by communally-identified 'men' being men, with the greater obligations of manhood.

It has very little to do with sexuality, something to do with gender in so far as it relates to gender roles rather than gender identification in itself, and a lot to do with a strict orthodoxy about the things that 'men' and 'women' are expected to do. Only a man can be a head of household. A head of household is essential, and now this person has risen to the obligation. Therefore, logically, this person must be a man.

That social context needs to be borne in mind when we contemplate Shote Galica wearing male clothing and fighting alongside the men, despite having a perfectly serviceable male around to do the male stuff. Some of the perception of her seems to mix a sense of the regrettable – she was deprived of the qualities of womanhood – and the unnatural: she was doing something peculiar and failing in both nature as well as womanly duty.

A 2014 article labelling her the 'Albanian Joan of Arc' suggested that her decision to accompany her husband showed not only her personal spirit but 'the great concept of spiritual emancipation that triumphs over the oppressive and patriarchal mentality regarding women' – what sociology professor Anna Di Lellio, looking at the famous photograph, calls 'the possible subversion of the patriarchal order through an egalitarian system of relationships forged in the rebellion against foreign powers'. But she goes on to point out that much of the Shote myth – the essential sense of unusualness – is actually about reinforcing gender stereotypes. Thus there is a set of distinctive and superior male virtues, and Shote was remarkable because she dared and was able to step up to them. Making a thing of how unorthodox she was only strengthens the predominance of the orthodoxy. At one point in one version of the stories – and these ought really to be read not as reportage from an early twentieth century conflict, but as folk tales – she has a scornful exchange with an enemy in which both present the wearing of women's clothes as a symbol of weakness. At another she 'disguises herself as a woman' – take a moment to unpack that thought – to be able to get close to an enemy officer she's trying to kill.

Others have suggested that she faced prejudice because she spent most of her time with the men. One of the more positive justifications for her enduring appeal in the twenty-first century is that she broke down barriers. This emphasises the extent to which, in her own time, what she was doing was seen not only as unusual but also as unnatural. Between the lines of the romantic legend are nuances of conventional reality: Azem had a second wife, and by some accounts a third. His wife Zoja – the name is also a dialect form of the word for 'lady' – was less inclined to make it into the war stories but able to produce a child.

It is almost impossible to find references to any wife other than Shote: perhaps a worthy reflection of her distinctive character and courage, but it emphasises how the only newsworthy activity is male. The superficial model of Shote's heroism – the frozen black and white defiance of the photograph – was adopted by Kosovo, which has needed icons in its fight against oppression, and then adopted by women for essentially the same reason. But this leaves unchallenged the structures into which she was co-opted, and leaves unspoken her private reality. In the old Albanian film portraying the epic of Azem and Shote, she is little more animated than in the photo: defiant, admirable, unusual – and silent.

In late 2020 there was a tiny Twitter spat around the identity and representation of Shote Galica. Vlora Çitaku – who herself went from war journalist, refugee and liberation army spokesperson to Government Minister and senior Ambassador – commemorated Shote as 'Fighter. Commander. Hero!' One experienced analyst and commentator replied, 'Also, mistress hence never wife [the marriage was never formalised], which in the temporal context and in Albanian literally equals to never woman. Upon her master's death, she was abandoned, miserable, homeless and died broken; she had no agency. We subscribe to Enver Hoxha's invention without any critique. … even when reaching the level of a hero, we still did not consider her a woman.' 'Have we failed to live up to her example?' asks Çitaku; 'that's our problem, not hers.'

As a woman who never had the education or opportunity she herself apparently believed in, to be able to articulate for posterity her own truth, Shote leaves unanswered the essential question about her instincts and motivation. Perhaps she really was the loyal partner and loyal patriot, who felt herself forced by circumstances to demonstrate those affiliations by following a path that was uncomfortable, unnatural and eventually fatal. Or perhaps her tragedy, solitary rather than shared, is that her own frustration or flexibility about her identity forced her onto a path of fighting and flight. (In which case perhaps it's not a tragedy at all, but a rare relative triumph of very private freedom.)

∽

Femrat – 'women' – is a stylish website 'where Albanian women can come together across the world and support one another'. With a stance unusually liberal in Albanian public discourse, it addresses 'contemporary issues such as gender, sexuality and society'. Femrat's tagline is 'Woman/Warrior/Shqiptarë [Albanian woman]'. Next to a stylised rendering of her face in the famous photo, now looking particularly stern, is the motto 'In Shote We Trust'.

In 'From Azem Galica to Shote Galica', published on the Femrat site in 2016, the poet Fortesa Latifi writes,

> '...even war is about love. Even love is about country.
> We are all fighting for the smallest of moments –
> to go home and drink strong tea in our own kitchens;
> to kiss our children's faces just as they are rising from sleep;
> to eat with our hands with three generations of family unfolded in the same room.'

Even today – the plaything of wilful and incoherent European Union policy and Russian manipulations, kept in constitutional limbo by international diplomacy at once both terribly clever and desperately clumsy – for a Kosovo Albanian, the struggle is for the right to a conventional domesticity. The ultimate symbol of the struggle's upheaval is that it forced the icon of domesticity, a woman, out of the kitchen and into combat.

Kosovo politician Jakup Krasniqi, who went from Liberation Army spokesman to speaker of Parliament, described in an article the educational benefit of Shote Galica's example, linking it explicitly to Xhevë Krasniqi Lladrovci. 'Not infrequently in our centuries-long history', he wrote, 'the Albanian woman has revealed her qualities as mother, as spouse, as teacher, as heroine, as leader and as steady-eyed warrior'. Can Albanian woman reveal more, between hearth-fire and gun-fire?

The site of Azem Galica's birth is almost as hard to find as that of his death. Hidden among the hills in the geographic heart of Kosovo, cradle of resistance at both ends of the twentieth century, is the village from which he took his name. It is a lovely drive to get there, a reminder of how beautiful Kosovo gets, the further you escape from the asphalt and the concrete. The increasingly winding and simple road passes frequent memorials to those killed fighting the oppressor in the late 1990s. In the village of Galica itself, an old man is escorting a very old man up the long hill. The latter – traditional felt hat, impressive moustache, deeply fissured face – is quietly eager to tell the family history and the story of Azem's restored stone house, *kulla*, and the graves around it. This is a bonus, because the *kulla* with its visitor information facility rarely seems to be open. The original *kulla*, or so the story goes, was dismantled in Yugoslav days when they needed the stone to build a new school in the adjoining village; but several years ago that school was being modernised and – perhaps a better advert for recycling than education – Galica village took all the stone back to restore Azem's home.

In a country still trying to escape Serbian provocations and international fiddling, it is sadly understandable that the warriors have captured the history as well as the politics, and that new generations still need to be raised to steady-eyed resilience. Even leaving aside those who have contributed to the fighting, Kosovo's women have done more than their fair share of the suffering. (And the commemoration of womanly endurance doesn't always extend to the many thousands of rape survivors from the war of 1999, whose violation by Belgrade's troops was followed with stigmatisation by their own community.)

A *New York Times* article of March 2021 suggested that a surge in successful women candidates in Kosovo's general election – winning nearly forty percent of seats – reflected 'growing discontent with the endemic corruption and bullying ways of a post-war order dominated by swaggering male veterans of the Kosovo Liberation Army'. Their success was despite – or because of – habitual and brutal discrimination in all aspects of political discourse: one male party leader predicted that traditional enemy Serbia would prefer a 'weak woman' in a leadership position to a strong man like him. The woman in question is now President of the Republic, so apparently the public are willing to risk a break with strong male leadership. In a remarkable combination of the Shote-like admiration for female embodiment of traditionally male virtues and the female need to stand up against male vices, a female activist described the appeal of one of the successful female candidates, a survivor of a wartime massacre, 'She is a survivor. She is strong as stone. She is our truth.' Another voter noted that 'She is stronger than all the men round here.' Albanian has a (feminine) noun which also serves as a popular female first name: Qendresa means something like endurance, resilience. This is a female virtue, and apparently a necessary one.

Must the most famous female name in Kosovan history be a district bandit? Despite the chaos, and the conflict, and the statelessness, and the systemic deprivation of education, and the patriarchy, other women have done other things. There have been female politicians, and doctors, and teachers, and writers, and actors. Yet 21st century Kosovan young women are still encouraged to trust in Shote. Their French contemporaries have Joan of Arc and Marianne, but they also have Marie Curie and Simone de Beauvoir. A British young woman might conceivably be inspired by the martial posture of Boudica and Elizabeth I, but is more likely to be pointed towards a Bronte or a Pankhurst for inspiration.

'Her name continues to represent the bravery and endurance of the Kosovan woman', says Lirie. Lirie is the 21st century Kosovo: an educated active professional, a psychologist and psychotherapist who gives up her free time to a low-cost clinic offering diverse counselling services. Yet hers is a generation in transition, within a country in transition. Kosovo has a kind of independence, but the international community prolongs the haggling over the country's status, and allows her people no voice in the UN. Kosovo's women, educated and determined, have won their professional freedom but not escaped traditional domestic expectations. 'Shote's behaviour was outside every possible expectation of that time: it was completely unheard of for a woman to line up beside the men in war, and consequently that kind of taboo-breaking meant that her story has lived on.'

Shote and Azem spent some time together in northern Albania; the famous photo of the couple was taken at the pioneering Marubi photographic studio, in 1920. In the city of Shkodra, it apparently became a proud boast to be able to say 'we saw Shote'. Seeing the renowned Amazon Shote – like seeing other distinctive or unusual creatures – was believed to be auspicious. Today the women of Kosovo are revealing their qualities not only as mothers, spouses, teachers, leaders (including two Presidents so far) and steady-eyed warriors (in the police and the nascent security force), but in every sector of professional and public life. Still they are fighting.

Chapter 7

Musine Kokalari
and the Albanian Silence

Alone among you pure I showed:
through your darkness strong I glowed,
to give you a little light;
to bring day out of night.

Albania's most distinguished woman writer spent the last decades of her life as a street sweeper. 'We were very isolated from everyone else,' Musine Kokalari said in an account recorded secretly in the early seventies. 'They would say no more than "hello" to us, and that was it.' Her secret police file contains a report that she has 'exchanged two or three words' with two other women in the street, and the informant is tasked to report if they meet again and what they say. When she died, her neighbours and fellow-internees were warned not to attend her burial. Her precocious distinction – in literature, in politics, in ethnography, and as a woman in society – was swallowed up by the ignorance and fear essential to Europe's most isolated and extreme communist regime.

The writer-politician Malëshova died a warehouseman. His funeral party comprised one relative and two secret policemen. Notoriously, if anyone dared speak to him, Malëshova would pinch his lips with his fingers. No one could be trusted. No word could be trusted. To say anything was to risk misrepresentation and betrayal.

The dictator Hoxha died just two years after Kokalari, and his cruel and bizarre regime fell seven years after her death. She is politely respected now: she was officially named a 'martyr of democracy', and a school was named for her, which in practice has always been Albania's highest honour as well as a handy benchmark for who's in favour. But the silence – the silence that swallowed her, the silence about what she really means to her country – endures.

The decades of Musine Kokalari's life followed a similar arc to the trajectories of Albania and of communism. Her youth was optimism and possibility; the disillusionment was bitter. She was born near the end of the First World War in what is now Turkey, but her family returned to their native Albania when she was very young. The country was in its infancy, still more an idea than an administrative reality. Seen from the outside, it was the most mysterious and backward extremity of Europe, the 'land of the living past' of Edith Durham who had explored it at the beginning of the century. 'The wanderer from the West stands awestruck… filled with vague memories of the cradle of his race.' Albanians (proudly) and foreigners (sniffily) have always defined Albania by its isolation, an untouched mountain people speaking an unalloyed proto-European language. In truth, the Albanian lands have always been a frontier, a place of exchange. Back when western Europe was an extremity, a marshy foresty pagan wildness at or beyond the edge of the map, the Albanian lands were at the geographic centre of the known world. Caesar fought Pompey for mastery of the Empire up and down the coastal strip, and his assassins were pursued to their doom along the great axis of the Roman Empire, the Via Egnatia, which ran across the territory. Caught between Rome and Venice and Vienna and Constantinople, the Albanians were for centuries the world's intermediaries: the traders and diplomats and warriors and spies. Chopped out of the crumbling Ottoman Empire in 1912, the new Albanian state was validated by the European Great Powers in 1913 at the Conference of London, and collapsed in 1914. It spent the First World War in a ravaged limbo, and its debris would have been parcelled out afterwards by the Powers but for the sponsorship of Woodrow Wilson, who insisted on its revitalised independence.

Albania has always been constructed as much from without as within. The politics and culture of the new state were the product of a diverse network of idealists and enthusiasts stretching across and beyond the old Ottoman Empire. Emigrants and re-immigrants from the Bosphoros to Boston dreamed and schemed. Albania's childhood in the 1920s was a jostling between the most progressive and sophisticated of European ideas and the feudal power politics of the mediaeval village, between poet-priests and mountain barons. This was Musine Kokalari's heritage and home. She was the product of a cultured and relatively cosmopolitan youth, in which the echoes of the 'Rebirth' movement of Albanian cultural nationalism only a generation before still resonated powerfully. Just before her

21st birthday she went to study literature in Rome, which was already offering an aggressive intrusive support to the new country, in the manner of a Caesar or a protection racketeer. She wrote her thesis on Naim Frashëri, one of a triumvirate of literary-political brothers, gods of the national awakening. He was an apt idol for an idealistic young writer. As an old woman, in isolation, she was still confiding her veneration of him to her notebooks.

I am the stars for which we strive;
I am the littlest thing alive.
I have the universe to show;
but who shall see the candle's glow?

(The extracts are from Frashëri's celebrated poem 'Fjalët e qiririt', in which a candle burns and speaks for and to the nation.) By the time Kokalari reached adolescence, a Turkish educated Vienna-imprisoned highland chieftain named Zogolli had survived factional chaos, shooting and exile to make himself Prime Minister, then President and eventually King. King Zog was the first modern ruler of Albania who could credibly claim control over anything like the full territory of the country, but he spent his reign trying to balance Italy's badly-needed investment with her more ambiguous political influence. Shortly after Kokalari arrived to study in Mussolini's Rome, Italy formally annexed Albania; within a year, the Second World War had begun. By the time Kokalari arrived home in 1941, Albania was under a puppet government and the war had reached neighbouring Yugoslavia and Greece.

Kokalari claimed that she wanted 'only to write literature, and to have nothing to do with politics'. While Albania endured occupation and the side-effects of the Second World War, and British parachutists were trying to spur resistance against the Italians and then the Germans, between 1941 and 1944 she published three volumes of folk tales in Tirana. This was writing in spite of the world, a glimpse of how it was possible to maintain a kind of normality and a kind of culture in the eye of the hurricane. Albanians have tended to see European politics through their own filter, and in the tortuous feuds of the republic, the monarchy, the occupied territory, the Communist fantasy and at last the new and brittle democracy, a few years' willingness to adapt to Italian and German occupation proved the least turbulent of transitions; wartime saw a brief realisation of the dream of more unified Kosovo and Albania. Or perhaps the folk tales – the explicit sentimentality and insubstantiality of the title *As My Old Mother Told Me* – were an escape. In a generation when Albania's male writers had tended to focus on patriotism and flirtations with modernism, a woman invoking her mother's store of folk tales was sticking to safe and sheltered ground.

It was reckoned, nonetheless, the first book written and published by an Albanian woman. Though her writing was deliberately nostalgic, Kokalari's political sense was already acute, active and progressive. The predominant importance of politics towards the end of the war would be forced on Kokalari's family in the most brutal way; for now she still found the urgency positive. The sense of opportunity, of a plurality of possibilities, is hard to imagine from the other end of the Cold War and the other end of the continent. (It was hard to imagine for the British soldiers who had parachuted in, trying to convince Albanian village headmen that they needed to pick a side, let alone the distant Allied one.) But Albania's monarchy had been short-lived, and Italian occupation would prove even shorter, and the Germans were already losing the war in Europe, and Enver Hoxha's partisans had yet to become as predominant or as absolutist as they would prove. Albania was a state half-formed, and for a brief hopeful moment, in the renewed rootlessness of war, political and poetical idealists had the chance to flourish. 'This word nationalism on its own can't capture the hearts of the peasants and the workers,' Kokalari insisted to a political acquaintance, 'even as a false hope. Stripped bare, the word nationalism belongs to the past, while the future demands social and economic change'. Before the war she'd already been publishing articles on social issues. She assisted with the *Gruaja Shqiptare* [Albanian Woman] magazine, writing under the name 'Tacita' – silent. It was partly an elaboration of her previous nom de plume, 'Muza'– a play on her own name, as well as the Albanian for 'muse' – but the Dea Tacita, the silent goddess, was the personification of obscurity, the divinity responsible for suppressing an unwanted voice. In 1943 she drafted the programme of a new Social Democratic Party, and was responsible for its newspaper, *Voice of Freedom*. As well as an independent united ethnic Albania, the party programme emphasised social justice and political freedom.

In a place that had had politics and politicians for no more than a generation, and remained patriarchal, the prominence of this woman in her twenties was remarkable. Perhaps the lack of a political tradition helped. Albania was young, and volatile, and hungry for influences. With fascism as the enemy, progressive politics was more appetising. But the same lack of political tradition made easy the rapid success of the Communistic partisan movement led by Enver Hoxha.

Albania's insular experiment in backwoods Stalinism would eventually crumble with the rest of the Eastern European regimes, at the end of the 1980s: a brittle oligarchy of old men who had been deft enough and mediocre enough to survive four decades of purges. Today, the movement's optimistic youth can only be glimpsed on the walls of one room of the National Gallery in Tirana: some of the socialist-realist pictures are glorious, with cheek-bones like Albanian mountains and colours fired by the national programme of electrification; some, in their adopted approved style, are very bad indeed. They all capture the energy of the movement, its pretence at universal popularity, its synthetic hope. In 1944 the partisan movement proved unstoppable: it had husbanded its strength during the occupation, refusing British prodding towards an active attritional guerrilla campaign, until the moment when Germany's fighting sap began to withdraw towards its core and the partisans could launch northwards over the country and fill the void; it offered enough socialism and optimism to inspire a people who had no alternative model of successful democracy to fall back on; it was ideologically coherent, stiffened by some discreet guidance from Yugoslav comrades, driven, focused, and – in out-of-the-way little massacres – ruthless.

The domestic opposition to the partisans was intermittently heroic, but negligible. The only other armed groups were a predominantly rural and northern gaggle, whose incoherence was confirmed by the diversity of labels attached to them, whose ideology was limited to general and diverse inclinations towards the way things used to be, and whose undoubted heroism was burned out in early half-cocked rebellions or exile. That left Musine Kokalari and her like: a tiny class educated enough to be able to perceive more than basic survival, and optimistic enough to believe that pluralism was possible. In November 1944, two of Kokalari's brothers were shot by 'liberation soldiers'. A third was spared – not because he'd been one of the dictator's classmates, but because he had a bad fever and the arresting party didn't want to pick him up. Musine herself was arrested a day later and interrogated, accused of provoking dissent by her advocacy of the Social Democratic movement. In elections at the end of 1945, the largely unopposed communists won 93% of the vote, and all of the seats in the new People's Assembly.

'Whatever pressure may have been brought to bear prior to the elections, during the voting no intimidation whatever was noticeable,' runs the report from the British Military Mission to Albania, now in the UK National Archives. In 1945, as today, the leaders of Albanian had accepted international observers of their election, as a handy external validation. 'In the North an air of boredom and bewilderment prevailed on voting day; in the South there was a cheerful atmosphere and in some localities drinking and dancing... It became apparent a week before the Elections that the Opposition lacked the courage, programme, organisational powers, unity and finally the time to express itself in any way.'

Buried in the complacency and generalisation was Musine Kokalari's supreme act of defiance, distinction and courage. In November 1945, in an atmosphere of suspicion and fear and hopelessness described powerfully in her secret account, a diverse group of non-Communists met furtively to discuss their predicament as elections loomed. On their behalf, Kokalari drafted and put her name to an appeal to the allies to push for a postponement of the elections, to give the various opposition groups time to muster credible alternatives to the communists. The note was passed to the British and the Americans and, taking a further risk, Kokalari pushed the point in a meeting with a British officer.

But this phase of the underwhelming history of British attempts to influence Albania according to some external principle or goal was ending. Just as Europe looks different from its opposite corner, so does its history. Britain had consistently failed to persuade any of the factions in Albania of the dubious proposition that they should pick a side in the World War, and risk their existence by early campaigns against the Germans as a contribution to the Allied effort rather than biding their time and concentrating on their own civil war. At every stage the British had pulled back from taking a decisive position, for fear that it would accelerate some undesired reaction – Italian entry to the war, the fall of Greece, open civil war in Albania – which in the end happened anyway and was probably inevitable.

By the end of 1945, Britain was trying to adjust to the new Albania; by the end of 1946, relations had been broken for good.

In the end, Britain could do nothing but burnish its role as spectator with the delusion that, one way or another, British influence had been decisive: the vain hope that British prompting and support could persuade the partisans to a more active role became the regretful myth that British support had enabled the partisan victory in the civil war; a few years later, the fantasy that infiltrating a few handfuls of British- and American-trained Albanian exiles might topple the Communist regime became the querulous assertion that the mission had only failed because of a British double-agent, Philby, rather than because of its inherent incompetence and futility.

As Kokalari said later, the British and Americans could at least have demonstrated that multi-party elections were important, and that opposition was in practice obstructed. But she was an inconvenient anomaly, something to be swept under the carpet as the foreigners tried to adjust to the new reality. (The clumsiness was mirrored in the early 1990s, when the western rush to support anything anti-Communist in Albania led to the validation of people and behaviours with short-term appeal but disastrous long-term consequences for the stability and political style of the country.) In the report on the 1945 elections, Britain's inability to do anything about what was happening in Albania was masked by elegant disdain for the opposition no-show. Musine Kokalari – and the possibility of democracy in Albania – became an anonymous aside, on a flimsy page in Kew. 'A small and unrepresentative clique signed a last minute petition to the British and American Governments to postpone and guarantee the elections. But the disgruntled elements in the State did not publicly contest the elections.'

~

Musine Kokalari disappeared into the silence. She was arrested in January 1946, just one among many in a wholesale assault on intellectuals and inconvenients. It is a familiar pattern; perhaps Albania's fragility made the long-term damage greater. Kokalari's speech at her trial was a triumph of defiance, of stubbornness in the face of ignorance and illegitimacy. The most famous photograph of her was taken at this apotheosis: the clothes are rough and monotone, the plain belted dress and the jacket and the scarf that frames her head; large eyes gaze up past the primitive microphone towards her judges, with something like insolence. A contrast with earlier pictures of her, their soft focus Sunday-best prettiness, the simple costume and dark beauty make this final image somehow timeless, and iconic. She was sentenced to twenty-five years in prison, and served sixteen. In the street outside the court, she was harassed by a warmed-up crowd.

A curious microcosm of Albania's isolation at the centre of the map, Burrel is not far from Tirana and the centre of the country, and yet buried many hours away behind mountains. Its prison was established in the time of King Zog for the most dangerous criminals, and it continues to fulfil that role more than ninety years and a few changes of political system later: the Prime Minister who opened it in 1938 died in it in 1949. Kokalari endured sixteen years there, and in 1962 was transferred to internment in the northern Albanian town of Rrëshen. Even today, after a generation of democracy and capitalism, and served accidentally by the impressive highway to Kosovo, Rrëshen is a bleak place: a tumble of plain barrack-like buildings, beside a mostly dry river-bed. Fifty years ago it was a forgotten purgatory, a place where life was scarce and rationed, hidden up a valley in an isolated, insecure and ever-suspicious land. The child of a trans-continental empire, nurtured in the culture of two great civilisations, Musine Kokalari was shrunk into a gagged recluse in a semi-closed provincial town. The diminishment says something of Albania's ever-narrower political perspective.

Still the flame burned. In 1972 she managed to complete her own secret account of the politics and ideals that had cost her her freedom, and which remained her inspiration. *The Birth of the Social Democratic Party* is both a chronicle of activism – that the erased names and furtive meetings and fateful signatures of those who strived in vain might not be lost to history – and a statement of belief. It's also, in its futility – a book written in secret and in the certainty that it could not be published for the foreseeable future – a powerful assertion that the essence of truth is that it exists, however obscured. When Kokalari was the focus of one of International PEN's first campaigns for the release of imprisoned writers around the world, Enver Hoxha – who as a schoolteacher in southern Albania had once sent complimentary letters to the student and published writer in Rome – said, 'Is that slut still alive?'

Kokalari lived alone, watched, haunted. A rare visitor to the town who asked after her was warned not to speak to her; her dossier has details of her slightest exchanges with others, and exhaustive instructions for how the movements and opinions of this abandoned old woman are to be tested; one report wonders whether a suspicious movement of her coat, and her carrying an umbrella, might not portend some anti-state activity. A worker in the town's tiny library was once phoned by the Secretary of the local Party Committee who had seen Kokalari sitting in front of a pile of books: the 'declassed old woman' must be hustled out of the library, forbidden to take anything to read. 'For the town, she was like a shadow.' The enthusiast for her nation's language and culture, the idealist for her people's rights and aspirations, the image of brave and scornful womanhood who dared to defy her judges: all of these Musines were buried. In this limbo, sweeping the streets, she lived a further twenty years.

∼

George Orwell began putting down ideas for what would become *Nineteen Eighty-Four* at around the time Musine Kokalari was writing her last appeal for pluralism, and by the time he finished she had vanished into the crude concrete barrack-cells of Burrel prison. The novel remains a startlingly effective insight on the rational nightmare of an extreme dictatorship like Albania, and it suggests that the most terrifying extensions of totalitarian control are over individual thought, and over the past.

The Hoxha regime exercised tight control over creative writing as well as news. Literary works would only be issued after a preliminary review of their political correctness, and might well be criticised harshly after publication. Either was dangerous for the author. It was not only risky to publish something controversial; it was almost impossible. A writer might think twice about writing something they knew to be inconsistent with political orthodoxy; they were obliged to worry whether something might possibly be, or subsequently become, interpreted as inconsistent. And when criticism can attach to stylistic as well as political incorrectness, it's easy to see how this kind of control breeds artistic mediocrity as well as conformity (or, as with the most widely-known Albanian writer, Ismail Kadare, a strong predisposition to allegory). The nature of the review and criticism process, and the possibility that official opinion might change over time, only increased the paranoia and danger around the creative act. When for example the novelist Sterjo Spasse, who in the thirties had produced the first great Albanian novel, was given the uncomfortable honour of delivering the general address to the 1966 Plenary of the League of Writers of Albania, his formulaic survey of the year's output was subsequently deemed to have been insufficiently harsh. His colleagues, including some who had signed off on his report before the event, were quick to add their condemnation of its shortcomings. The old man's writings and utterances came under increased scrutiny, and even then he was luckier than some of that year's writers, who were formally condemned in public and workplace meetings across the country and sent to labour camps to learn greater familiarity with reality.

A recent exhibition of the writing of Ismail Kadare included examples of how censorship worked under the Hoxha regime. Manuscripts of his new novels submitted for publication show the corrections required by the system, but so too do copies of previously-published works: if for example a work had referred to a political or cultural figure who had since fallen from favour, the offending name has been scrubbed out, and the section was to be re-written for a new edition. This is what Orwell has his protagonist, Winston Smith, doing in *Nineteen Eighty-Four*: forever rewriting historical documents so that the archival record remains consistent with the latest political context. History, and literature, and the history of literature change to conform to the present.

Musine Kokalari never even had the chance to endure this system: she was shut up in her prison behind the mountains before the regime was a year old. But even now that the regime has fallen, the liberation of suppressed and dissident voices has been limited.

There's a school named after Musine now, and a museum in her hometown, and a library – though in a recent visit the library, like her, didn't have any books. But Albania's preliminary attempts at coming to terms with its Communist past have been wary, and uncomfortable. Many of the organised events turn into angry speeches by old men and women, to each other, bitter that their stories and their truths are still unheard. After the fall of the Communist regime a few of its surviving figureheads were given short prison sentences, but there has been no systematic process against those who prosecuted, those who framed, those who judged, those who tortured. 'We know who they are!' complains one speaker at a centenary conference on Kokalari, to an audience of frustrated fellow-survivors. A constituted agency is now responsible for managing access to the old secret police files – those that weren't burnt – but interest in them is more concerned with gossip or today's feuds. There's an institute explicitly for studies into the crimes of Communism, but its head was forced out and into exile in 2019 after a defamation campaign neatly redolent of the character assassinations that typified Communist prosecutions; the system, he noted in an interview published in the *Symbol* literary journal in 2021, 'is like a snake, which sloughs off its old skin in the spring' and endures, and he pointed out that the last Interior Minister of the Communist regime was the current Speaker of Parliament.

Albania's brand of paranoid totalitarianism depended on everyone being willing to denounce their neighbour, their friend, or their parent. A substantial proportion of the population found it necessary, or possible, to implement this. How do you apportion guilt – what is guilt? – when everyone was complicit? One former political prisoner suggests that it's all about – and has always been about – control of property; the descendants of distinguished families of the 1920s are pursuing Kafkaesque legal procedures for the restitution of property usurped under fascism, and again under Communism and again under corrupt capitalism. Wholesale compensation for property seized by the regime would be too expensive, and decisions about property are too profitable to be left to a truly efficient and impartial judicial process. On the foundations left by the Ottoman and Communist societies, a wild west frontier capitalism has been built. Communism made selfishness essential to survive; capitalism has made selfishness essential to succeed. The inconvenient truths of history are irrelevant, unhelpful, and forgotten.

Someone like Kokalari can now be politely venerated, because she represents abstract virtues and is safely dead. Some of the people who prosecuted her and the people who harangued her in the street and the people who tormented her during her long isolation are still alive, in an Albania which seems tacitly to have decided to let bygones be bygones. Least said soonest mended, and the elderly ex-prisoner of the regime may still bump into their torturer on the street corner.

Forty years after her death, Kokalari's work and voice are no longer actively suppressed. Albania's political leaders no longer curse that she hasn't died, but instead offer her honours now that she has. She exists more than she seemed to between 1946 and 1983. But it's not clear that she speaks and is heard. For Dr Lori Amy, a scholar of the country's failure to engage meaningfully with its past, to truly hear Kokalari we should acknowledge how the dictatorship came to power, how it stayed in power, and how elements of that model of power have been neither expunged nor properly examined. To hear Musine Kokalari, we must hear that young voice of curiosity and optimism, and we must hear the worldlier voice of political urgency, and we must hear the lonely old voice that continued to think and to create.

Even that haunting image of her in the courtroom – the victim, frozen into beauty, mouth closed, waiting – is defined by silence, passivity, victimhood. She is an icon rather than a voice, seen but not heard. As scholar Agata

Fijalkowski notes in a study of the famous photo, 'while her image has been accorded a key part in the prevailing historical and political narratives about the country's Communist history, her own account of her life, and the accounts given by others, are still swathed in silence'. It is the fact that she was a woman and the first woman writer that distinguishes her today, not what she wrote.

In her isolation, forbidden to write publicly, watched suspiciously by everyone, Musine Kokalari confided her ideas and her enthusiasms to dozens of cheap paper notebooks, supplemented with reused scraps of receipt or list. In painfully economical tiny handwriting, she gathered her reflections and her research into folk culture, and language, and literature. Through 37 years of solitude, it was impossible for her lively mind not to think and to write, though she knew that her work could not be read. Carefully guarded by one of her relatives, two small suitcases of notebooks are all that is left of Musine Kokalari.

You have still so much to learn
while I, yet silent, burn.

Chapter 8

The Voice Outside:
Esma Redžepova

The costumes of the band are pantomime gypsy: bright plain or paisley shirts and little waistcoats. They start to play with melodramatic mournfulness, trumpet and sax conducting the lament as they sway, the accordion wringing pain out of his face as well as his squeeze-box, a wild-haired double-bass bent low over his bow.

A woman stands among them, short and almost round. She is draped in fabric – voluminous pantaloons, a blouse with billowing sleeves, a gorgeous waistcoat, scarves, a rich cloth wound round her head and folding down the side.

During 2010, America's National Public Radio produced a list of the 50 greatest voices ever recorded, one a week, everyone from Maria Callas to Freddie Mercury. Eleventh on the list – just after Ella Fitzgerald, slightly before Nat King Cole – was a folk singer from Macedonia.

Esma Redžepova is glorious in red and gold, a comic-book pasha, a buddha. The audience, rapt, reverent, waits.

Slowly, slightly, she opens her mouth and starts to sing.

~

Esma Redžepova was born in 1943, in Skopje – today the capital of North Macedonia. Her father was a musician; she was one of six children. In 1956, when she was in her early teens, a teacher persuaded her to enter a music competition run by Radio Skopje. According to her later telling of the story, she hadn't dared tell her parents because they wouldn't have approved.

She won. So she then had to hide eleven million Yugoslav dinars in her underwear. (Or a different large number of dinars; the figure would vary dramatically between tellings over fifty years. Lots of dinars, anyway.) Her mother found the money, the equivalent of months of salary, a couple of days later. 'She exploded at once. And when my father came home, she explained to him and he was a little angry.' Even a musician was sceptical about his daughter going into music.

Her success on the radio had another and more lasting consequence. One man who heard it was Stevo Teodosievski, already established in the mid-1950s on the radio and as a band-leader. His parents had been even less impressed by music, and as a boy he'd earned a few forbidden coins singing at the local bar. To him the voice on the radio show sounded 'like a silver bell,' and he visited her family to persuade the parents of this precocious talent that they should allow him to take their daughter away to a musical career. She had to promise her father 'that if I became a singer, I would only be a radio singer – I'd never play in restaurants or bars or something like that' – the even less reputable end of the profession. Teodosievski had her study for two years at the Academy of Music in Belgrade, and then she joined his ensemble.

It was the beginning of a high-profile singing career that would last more than fifty years. In 1961 she recorded her first album with the Ensemble Teodosievski, including a song she'd written herself when she was nine. 'Čaje Šukarije' – a song written by a little girl, about a little girl – would appropriately enough become one of her signature pieces.

Little girl, pretty one, don't walk so slow behind me,
don't walk so slow behind me, girl!
You have devoured and burned me,
you have stolen my heart,
turn, look at me, girl!

Redžepova and Teodosievski married in 1968. The Ensemble's renown coincided with the spread of television, and during the sixties Esma Redžepova won national prominence. In the seventies it would become global. Yugoslavia was a central player in the Non-Aligned Movement of states trying to survive in the middle of the Cold War. Mrs and Mr Teodosievski and their group toured not only all round Europe, but North and Central America, the Warsaw Pact and Soviet Union, the Middle East and Asia and even Australia. Esma sang for Indira Gandhi, Muammar Ghaddafi and the Shah of Iran.

In Tito's multi-ethnic Federation, folk music was safely sentimental, usefully inclusive, and literally popular. Redžepova sang in almost all of the Federation's different languages. The confected Yugoslavia – a second attempt at unifying a set of peoples who were ethnically and linguistically closely related, but had spent a millennium in and out of their own and other people's kingdoms

– was perpetually trying to balance the challenges of its precarious international position between East and West, and those of its fragile internal cohesion. During the sixties, the regime was losing heart in its efforts to foster a coherent Yugoslav culture, and accepting a diversity grounded in the peoples and republics that made up the federation. This empowered more strident and divisive voices, which the regime felt it had to tolerate even if it could not be comfortable with them. The public, meanwhile, less keen than their ideologues to abandon the reassurance and relative stability of the Yugoslav model, continued to cling to unifying cultural elements. A music that did not represent too strongly any particular modern trend, nor any particular modern identity, was less likely to tip the balance. And it allowed its audience to escape challenges, into something older and safer and familiar.

Accordingly, Esma never really went out of fashion, in as much as she was ever in it. (When the producers of the 2006 comedy *Borat* were looking for a song that sounded stereotypically folky, to illustrate the primitive rusticity of their Kazakhstan, they got legal permission to use Redžepova singing 'Čaje Šukarije'. They didn't get *her* permission though, and she successfully sued her production house.) As the music world moved from rock'n'roll to punk to pop, she merely solidified – in every sense – her image as an icon of national fondness, as people clung to the unchanging old things with affection. Yugoslavia died during the 1990s, and Stevo Teodosievski in 1997. But as the twentieth century passed into the twenty-first, Esma moved from maternal to grand-maternal status back home in newly-independent Macedonia.

As her fame had grown, she had begun to represent something more than music alone. She and Teodosievski – who never had children of their own – established an unusual mix of fostering and mentoring. They founded a music school, and shepherded nearly fifty disadvantaged boys through it. The accounts are vague about how much they were formally adopted and fostered. Redžepova called them 'my children', Teodosievski his 'successors' who would keep the ensemble going after him; a number did indeed perform with their 'mama'. Redžepova sponsored benefit concerts and worked for refugees from Kosovo. In 2002 she was nominated as United Nations Ambassador for Refugees in Macedonia, and her country twice nominated her for the Nobel Peace Prize. Increasingly, the grand old woman of folk music was adopted as a political voice and token. She became a member of the governing party, and in her late sixties was twice elected to Skopje city council.

In the era of Yugoslavia and Non-Alignment, the foreign tours were a celebration of how culture could reinforce trans-nationality: within the Federation, in its international network, in the world of folk music. During and after Yugoslavia's collapse in the 1990s, culture was required to celebrate nationality. When she represented Macedonia in the 2013 Eurovision Song Contest – at the age of 69 – Redžepova's initial offering was deemed too obnoxious a celebration of the then-government's nationalistic posturing; the song 'Empire' was replaced by 'If I Could Change the World', but that didn't get beyond the semi-final.

She died in 2016. Her funeral was a national mourning, attended by politicians and celebrities; Skopje's mayor described her as 'a queen of humanity, who represented Macedonia around the world'. One newspaper described the ceremony 'Sending the Queen to sing to the angels'.

∼

The concept of being Macedonian is complicated, and often controversial. It has changed over the centuries. It has changed since we started writing this chapter. As ever in the Balkans, it never helps to start a discussion with a clear set of borders in mind (nor to expect to finish it with them).

The Macedonia of Alexander the Great was centred to the south of the country that currently incorporates the name, though his victories carried him up into it. The Roman Macedonia covered a wider area, though today's country was similar to the bit they charmingly hived off as *Macedonia Salutaris*, 'Wholesome Macedonia'. It was successively part of the Byzantine, Bulgarian, Serbian and finally Ottoman Empires. The area was taken by Serbia again after the Balkan Wars, and then Bulgaria again during the First World War. It was then incorporated into the Kingdom of Serbs, Croats and Slovenes, which became the first Yugoslavia, and after another World War (briefly Bulgarian again) it was regathered into Tito's Yugoslavia.

But while the area remained part of something(s) else, the term 'Macedonian' had re-acquired political meaning. Efforts had begun during the late nineteenth century to establish an autonomous Macedonia within the Ottoman Empire; many of the movement's activists had Bulgarian roots, affinity and eventually support. With the restoration of Serbian dominance after 1913 and again after 1918, there was an official campaign to root out Bulgarian political and cultural influence – even in names. An activist movement endured: its name went through various evolutions, usually including 'Macedonian Revolutionary Organisation', and its approach mixed guerrilla resistance, gangsterism, terrorism and a recognised specialism in assassination. When, forty years after Tito had suppressed the movement, a new state of Macedonia voted itself out of the collapsing Yugoslavia and into independent existence, a new generation of nationalists adopted the old name for their political party.

To the Slavs who are the majority of the population of the country, and who would almost invariably call themselves Macedonian, it has seemed a vulnerable identity. For generations, more than one neighbour claimed ownership of Macedonia's land, language and identity, and those instincts linger. Its current borders have now been agreed – if not entirely – for seventy years or so, but in the past it has had other borders, or none, for much longer. It has been a country for some thirty years – within the lifetime of many of its citizens.

The name 'Macedonia' was consistently disputed by Greece, which prefers that term to refer to the larger and more southerly region more congruent with Alexander's ancient kingdom and the modern Greek administrative district which have both carried the name. Greece treated Macedonia's attempt to be called Macedonia as a statement of aggressive intent. Macedonia treated Greece's attempt to reject the name as a statement of aggressive intent. A generation of documents and discussions generated by international organisations, where Greece tended to be more influential, had to refer to the Former Yugoslav Republic of Macedonia. Because my enemy's enemy is my friend, a generation of international documents had to carry a footnote declaring that Turkey recognised the Republic of Macedonia under its constitutional name. After protracted internationally-mediated negotiations with Greece, the country acquired the name 'North Macedonia', recognised by international agreement and national referendum. Acceptance was certainly not unanimous, and political and nationalistic controversy continued. North Macedonians know that a significant element of their identity can change by popular whim or international pressure.

International insecurity has been echoed and exacerbated by internal insecurity. More than a quarter of the population is ethnically Albanian, speaking Albanian as well as Macedonian, and many living in relatively homogeneous areas abutting the predominantly ethnic Albanian neighbour countries of Albania and Kosovo. In 2001, ethnic Albanian guerrillas fought an insurgency against the authorities, fighting for greater recognition of rights and autonomy at least, and perhaps for secession. Those for whom Macedonia and being Macedonian mean something have had to come to terms with a community among their fellow citizens for whom being Macedonian means something rather different, and who might be willing to carve off a chunk of Macedonia and make it something else.

This enduring fragility has given extra force to identities that endure, and identities that transcend identity. Esma Redžepova was born before Macedonia. Two generations knew her and her songs through the transition from autonomous Macedonia-in-Yugoslavia to independent Macedonia, and a third generation grew up with her under independence. The repertoire, and the singer, expanded and adapted; but the essence did not change. It remained something familiar. Esma and 'Čaje Šukarije' and the rest had been part of their culture for as long as most could remember, and they remained so.

The evolution was not from being Yugoslav to being Macedonian, becoming less one thing and more another. For Esma the Yugoslav-ness she had borne so successfully seems more like a coat that, in due season, she took off. By the turn of the millennium, she was perceived and presented as a Macedonian icon: to the Eurovision judges, to the Nobel committee, to the Skopje voters. She herself said in 2006, 'I represent Macedonia everywhere in the world, and my ambassador mission is to present my country to its best.' Today, Macedonians feel that Esma Redžepova is theirs, in a way that none of the other bits of the former Yugoslavia do.

∼

Esma Redžepova's impact – her status as national treasure, her global prominence, the peculiar diversity of her renown – was remarkable enough. What makes her the unlikeliest of icons is that she was Roma; one of Europe's outcasts. Paradoxically, her race was both an enormous challenge, and at the same time essential to her identity as a musician.

The Roma people have been nomads and outcasts for a millennium and a half, since they first migrated west from India. The first extant reference to them in Europe, from the fourteenth century, described them as Sons of Cain: the original criminal and exile. They've also been described as the descendants of Abel, the wanderer feared and hated by the settled man. Today the majority of the world's Roma are in Europe, especially the south-east, though there are a couple of million in the Americas.

As outsiders, travellers, and distinctively darker-skinned, they were multiply strange to the settled peoples of mediaeval western Europe. Over the centuries they were periodically and consistently abused, enslaved, expelled, and/or slaughtered. A supplement to the Nazi Nuremberg Laws declared the Roma 'enemies of the race-based state', and by the mid-1930s they were already being interned in camps, with serious discussion of their wholesale removal. (Their geographic and racial origin, of course, made them more likely descendants of the real Aryans than most Nazis were.) In central Europe and the Nazis' Balkan satellites, the Holocaust – it has various names in Roma communities, including 'the devouring' – murdered somewhere between a couple of hundred thousand and a million and a half Roma, 25-75% of the diverse assessments of the European Roma population of the time. The very uncertainty of the scale of slaughter reflects how marginal the Roma existence has always been to official societies.

A 2019 exhibition at London's Wiener Holocaust Library referred to the Roma as the 'forgotten victims' of the Holocaust. In the twenty-first century they continue to exist on or beyond the margins of settled consciousness, of bureaucratic legitimacy, of tolerance. Official studies show a pattern of wholesale discrimination and exclusion. The European Union had to put improved treatment of Roma among its conditions for potential new member states, recognising that

> 'Roma communities suffer from social and cultural exclusion in most European countries... The problems most commonly faced by Roma populations are racism and discrimination, low levels of education, high unemployment (50-90%), health standards well below those of the mainstream population, and very poor housing conditions.'

When infant mortality – the number of children who do not live to their first birthday – was 3 per 1,000 in the UK, and 12 per 1,000 in Kosovo, among Kosovo's Roma it was 41 per 1,000. Certain words recur through Amnesty International's press releases about the Roma: eviction, segregation, discrimination.

The practical realities are clearer on the fringes of Balkan towns. These are the poorest countries in Europe, and their poorest citizens are generally the Roma. They exist in shanty-towns, rough breeze-block houses or mad improvisations of containers and cast-off wood and plastic sheeting. Even those Roma who get lucky will build and plaster their elaborate two-storey house in the Roma quarter. In each place, the name of the main Roma settlement is treated as a byword for poverty, pollution, risk. International development workers mutter the names with macho awe: a challenge to health, determination and the standard theories of economic empowerment. Locals may never even mutter them: themselves hardly affluent, they will go a lifetime without visiting or even being aware of the grim conditions just a kilometre or two from their funky cafes. Roma exist out of sight and so out of mind: they live on the edge of town; by unspoken agreement they sit at the back of the bus; those Roma children who do attend mainstream school will be consigned to the back row. They beg, or they search through the communal rubbish bins for plastic and metal to sell on to a recycling middle-man; a good day's haul from the bins, wheeled away in gigantic sacks strapped precariously to bike or wheelbarrow then sold by weight, will earn a handful of euros in a day.

The non-Roma may only see the Roma at the cross-roads, by the bins, or slumped on a bit of cardboard in the pedestrian area with their hands out. They will only notice them through music.

As much as the world has always found the Roma – the gypsies – frightening and distasteful in every aspect of life but one, so in the one that reaction is powerfully adapted or even reversed. In art, someone to fear turns into someone thrilling, someone attractively mysterious, someone transgressively exciting. The squeegee-boy at the traffic-lights ignoring the panicked refusals of the drivers becomes Heathcliff. The girl with one hand holding her baby to her chest and the other through your car window becomes Esmeralda. A Roma casual labourer/smuggler with a knife is, as Mérimée and Bizet showed, worth ruining your life over if she's got rhythm and a fiery soprano.

For the Roma of the Balkans, music has been the path to pride, status, relative wealth – and some acceptability outside their own community. For a people forced to live communally – big families, small spaces – group music is a more natural art form than sculpture or novel-writing. For a people whose literacy levels have remained terribly low, and who have generally been excluded from mainstream institutions of learning, music is how stories and histories are recorded and recounted.

Roma music is celebration, and families who would be horrified at marrying into the Roma would be glad to have their music at a wedding ceremony. Music is lament, the echoes back and forth between an individual's ache of love and a folk memory of oppression. Music is the best way, or the only way, to earn some money from others. Roma music is frenzied violins, or a mad explosion of brass, or a dancing guitar, or a bubble-gum confection of pop mysticism and synthesisers, or the thump of drums under ancient voices of endurance, or the solitary voice of a woman, gliding round and whirling you up into the dance. 'There is no Gypsy existence without music', accordionist Chico Iliev says in *Princes Amongst Men*, Garth Cartwright's passionate punk road-trip through the diversity and life of musicians including Esma and many others, 'The music is our medicine; our opium.' Esma's song 'Esma's song' suggests that music is an escape from life's suffering, that it 'brings sweetness to the soul'. 'Music is the only luxury of the poor', she told one interviewer, 'one of our rare pleasures which costs nothing. It brought some brightness into our dreary lives, it saved us some humiliation…When you sing you have no evil thoughts and when you are dancing you feel less hungry.'

'Gypsy' men and women were stereotyped as wilder and more passionate, the flip-side of their perceived primitiveness and inability to conform. Their fragile, flexible, itinerant life could be presented – if only in fiction, or in the fantastical philosophical pseudo-memoirs of George Borrow – as a model of greater freedom than conventional citizens knew. 'Through Zemfira's wild, dark eyes,' Pushkin notices in 'The Gypsies', 'another world of freedom lies'. And their music has been seen in the same way: less restrained, more of the heart. To listen to Roma music, to be caught up in its fire, is both dangerous dalliance with the other and an embrace of something lurking in oneself. For Carmen, epitome of danger and desirability, there's a direct link between emotional and legal unrestraint, and a singing gypsy is its embodiment:

> 'Passion is a gypsy child –
> one never bound by law.
> Love me or not, I'll love you wild;
> fear it, you whom I adore.'

Esma was no Carmen: her parents, her TV producers and her own nature would never have allowed that. But the relatively genteel audiences on Yugoslav radio and TV were seeking and enjoying a shadow of the wild fireside. (They were both the readers of Pushkin and the audience he describes, 'The old man leans upon his staff,/ and softly beats the tambourine./ Aleko, singing, leads the bear./ Zemfira takes what folk can spare/ and gladly from each passing scene.') Through music the Roma can represent their own world most vividly, but also reach the other world beyond the mahala. 'A chance to be something different', says Kosovan Roma musician Jimmy Mustafa of the tradition. Through the same music the non-Roma can pretend to be more exotic than they really are, and more accommodating of the existence of the Roma in their world. 'Someone who doesn't want to think or hear about problems of Roma,' says Jimmy, 'he listens to Roma music.'

So when Esma Redžepova decided to become a singer, it was hardly unprecedented; her father had been a musician, of course. It was a well-trodden path, and she had few others. But that didn't make it easy or uncontroversial. Remember her need to assure her parents that she wouldn't be singing in bars or restaurants – precisely the kinds of places where, outside community events, she was most likely to be singing. That her path was recognised didn't make it any less comfortable for her parents. But something new was happening in her generation. Together with Yugoslavia's promotion of a more diverse culture, radio and then television were making singing, particular popular singing, a more general experience: less intimate, less event-specific, less community-specific. Something that previously you could only have heard had you gone to the sorts of weddings or the sorts of bars where Roma music played, you could now hear in your own home, or in the austere and artificial ritual of the TV studio. Even by the end of Esma's life, the Roma had not escaped the discrimination or the mahala; but she had helped spread the music and what it represented.

There was yet another aspect to the challenge. Music may have been a recognised speciality of the Roma, and an established path, but it was still unusual and controversial for a woman. Contrary to the fantasies of centuries of non-Roma poets and composers, Roma women have often existed in a conservative set of social expectations. Redžepova was trying to sustain a success that depended on being appealing, but was always measured against what was appropriate – as a Roma, as a woman, as a woman in public. She claimed credibly to have been the first Roma performer to sing Roma songs in the Roma language, outside closed Roma events. Over sixty years she had to navigate a social and cultural context which was constantly evolving, but never ceased to be defined by restraints: racism, conservatism. In doing so, she helped that tradition evolve. 'She raised female arts to a level of respectability', according to scholar of Roma culture Carol Silverman, 'by playing with images of emotionality and sexuality.' Marrying a fellow-musician was a charming development in a professional relationship, but it was also the only way in which Esma would be able to continue singing in public. (That's not to suggest any cynicism in the decision, which as a mixed marriage was almost unprecedented and brought significant criticism for each of them from their respective communities.) Moreover – and again not implying any particular causation – the fact that she continued to have a public professional career and the fact that she did not become a mother are not unrelated. Her talent and adaptability, working with Stevo and beyond, enabled her to cross the boundaries of the Roma musical tradition in Yugoslavia. In her repertoire, her backing musicians, her costumes, she bridged its different national traditions, combined East and West, endured. Overcoming her various vulnerabilities – as a

Roma, as a woman, and then as an ageing Roma woman in a volatile cultural and political arena – she maintained her authenticity as a person and a performer, and fostered her legitimacy within the diverse traditions in which she had to operate.

In 1976, Redžepova took her music home, for the ultimate Roma family celebration. Her people had begun to leave India more than a thousand years before; in 1976 the first World Festival of Roma Songs and Music was held in Chandigarh. Esma was invited by Indira Gandhi, and she and Stevo were named Queen and King of Roma Music. (A moment to remember Stevo's journey and achievement too: the non-Roma who had a vision that Roma music could become acceptable and successful, who guided and encouraged and protected the young Esma, and himself overcame considerable prejudice.) Meanwhile, her charity and social work had a very strong Roma focus: not only the ensemble and the fostering, but also a women's association, a museum, an archive, a clinic.

Cultural tokens – like all symbols of identity – provoke fierce jealousy. The Bulgarian documentary film-maker Adela Peeva told the story of a supper with a cross-section of Balkan friends, when the band started playing a traditional song – and each of her friends claimed it as originally from their country. In her film *Whose Is This Song?* (2003), Peeva travels round the Balkans – including Turkey and Greece – confirming that each country does indeed know it as traditional and personal. The suggestion to any one of them that the song might belong equally or originally to one of the neighbours provokes variously scorn, anger, and near lynching. Despite her proud celebration of her

Romani heritage, and despite her later association with nationalist politics, Redžepova put the performance before the politics. At times she was criticised by Roma activists for indulging in stereotypes of 'gypsy' music, at times for suppressing the identity for palatability or pop credibility. Perhaps part of her strength and her durability was that, as a singer already recognisably 'other' – colourfully other, tolerably other – she was more adaptable, adoptable and acceptable.

～

She opens her mouth and starts to sing.

What comes out is more sound than words, and it's fatuous to try to describe sound in words. For those who never had the chance to see Esma live, YouTube has clips of her singing 'Gelem, Gelem' and 'Čaje Šukarije' and much else. Her obituary in the New York Times described her voice as 'a caldron of emotions. It could be a raspy shout, a sob, a nuanced tease, a model of long-breathed purity or an invitation to dance'; to the Washington Post, it had sounded 'like a beat-up Mustang barreling along a street full of potholes: it's gamy and battered and tough and it's been places'.

A few miles out of the capital of Kosovo is Gračanica, a town with a Unesco World Heritage monastery and a population that's on the whole ethnically Serb; it has a chic hotel with a multi-ethnic management and staff, and every Sunday two or three Roma lads come and sit in the hotel garden and sing a few songs: simple, beautiful, just voice and guitar. They are the Jimmy Mustafa Band – and you can find them on YouTube, Apple Music and Instagram, as well as over your Gračanica brunch. When he's asked about Esma, Jimmy is immediately enthusiastic and devoted. He and his mate remember being part of a concert with her in 2005, they a couple of teenagers and she at the height of imperial fame. 'She was very kind to us'; he sounds amazed, and a bit proud. What was so special about her? 'Her voice.'

In the older, black-and-white footage that's available, from back when she was of a more conventional age to sing the songs of a young lover, her voice and movements are more restrained. The concerns of her parents about singing in public were much more recent then, and it's as if she's still being careful. In the more modern footage, with lurid technicolour probably more suited to her costumes, she's naturally a much more confident and active performer. She flirts with the musicians, and she flirts more with the sounds they produce.

Then her own voice joins like an instrument in its own right. Words are stretched and evolved into nothing, into pure sound. They can barely be distinguished as words, a kind of maternal complacency breaking into moan of grief, and the audience doesn't care. It's irrelevant that she's an unlikely figure to be singing in 'Čaje Šukarije' about her unrequited passion for a young girl, because that's not what folk songs and this folk song are about. Her audience have accepted and adopted the song as something familiar, and then something both personal and shared; and so they have accepted and adopted the singer, and she has transcended her identity and become beloved. It's irrelevant that when she sings 'Gelem, Gelem', most of her audience are more likely descendants of the Roma's oppressors.

Esma became something broader than her own identity, and something less specific: it was an extraordinary achievement, and ambiguous, and it remains more resonant for the Roma. 'She is our queen', says Jimmy the Roma singer. 'She is our mother.'

Thanks

It will be clear from references in the text just how many people have contributed with research and support to the essays here. Some, mentioned in the text, gave us professional or practical support or just a badly-needed drink of blueberry juice. Some are quoted, and we appreciate their engagement and expertise. We would also like to thank Fjori Artemisiu, and Veronika and Ivana Trimpalik for support on travels in Albania and Montenegro; Besa Berberi and Edit Pula for transport and excellent company to Galica; Jelena McCoy for help with researching Maga Magazinović in Belgrade; Sihana Nebiu and Igor Parnadjiev for thoughts on Esma Redžepova; and Andy McGuffie and Gentiana Murati Kapo for ongoing ideas, practical help and friendship as we researched in Sarajevo.

We have tried to be precise in ascribing our sources, but we have deliberately not freighted the book with footnotes or end-notes for the many and diverse written and digital references we have consulted. Exact references are available, and we would be very grateful to know if we seem to have missed an attribution in the text.

Special gratitude to the Belgrade City Museum for allowing us to use the stunning photograph on the cover – and to Su Jones and Paddy McEntaggart for incorporating it into a great design, and to Sally Ellis-Rudd for making plain text look so much more.

Throughout the writing, Elizabeth has felt supported and helped with useful feedback by the Itinerant Writers Group and by Aparna, Cathy, Janet, Lynne, and Rachel of her weekly co-working group. Thank you!

And all this is nothing to the teamwork that will be needed by women and men; by governments and civil society; by the extraordinary and the ordinary coming together if we are to tackle some of the many and varied challenges described in these essays. These are challenges faced in the Balkans and beyond by women and girls every single day – at home, at work; in public life as in their most intimate relationships. In taking on these challenges, we take inspiration from role models from history, and we look forward to a future when we don't need such role models: when their work is done.

During the writing of this book, we took on a significant new identity which we're very proud of: we were invited to take part in the traditional first hair-cutting ceremony that made us *ndrikulla* and *kumbar* (translating loosely as 'godparents' or 'sponsors') of little Diella Berisha. Having already had eleven years inspired by her sister, Adena, whose hair we were also the first to cut, we feel the weight of responsibility we took on with this new role. But most of all, it's given us one more reason to hope and work for the Balkans – and beyond – to become a place where girls can dream and plan to be whatever they want; where they will be safe; where their voices will be heard; where they can offer their intelligence, their work and their talents – their love and their creativity – to the world, knowing their contributions will be welcomed and respected; and where we will all benefit as a result.

Also by Elizabeth Gowing

Travels in Blood and Honey:
becoming a beekeeper in Kosovo

When, in 2006, Elizabeth is told she is moving to Kosovo, the name of her new home conjures up blood: ethnic cleansing and war. This book reveals another side to what she found in the newest country in Europe – a land of generous families, strong tastes and lush landscapes: a land of honey.

Geraldine Doogue of Australia's ABC Radio National described the book as being 'about beekeeping, belonging and the business of politics but it's also a book rich with history and recipes, and insights about language and learning.'

The Times calls it 'a sheer delight; a beguiling, bittersweet story of a lively love affair with a traditional world, as ancient as apiculture, in transition to new nationhood'

Edith and I:
on the trail of an Edwardian traveller in Kosovo

In 1900 Europe's last wilderness was explored by a stout, stubborn English-woman who travelled in her tam o'shanter across Albania's Accursed Mountains. One hundred years later, Elizabeth Gowing follows Edith Durham's trail into Kosovo, finding not only an Edwardian heroine but also a guide for today.

The Rubbish Picker's Wife:
an unlikely friendship in Kosovo

How can you find the best rubbish pastures for scavenging? How can you free children to go to school rather than to go out begging? Can mayonnaise deal with headlice? An account of an extraordinary charity, and the challenges and delights of finding your community a long way from home.

The Silver Thread:
a journey through Balkan craftsmanship

From the mines in the cantos of Dante, to the prizes stolen in the wars of the nineties, follow the silver thread through Balkan history and culture to the new generation of craftswomen facing their uncertain future.

Unlikely Positions in Unlikely Places:
a yoga journey around Britain

Elizabeth Gowing is not a likely yogini. She is too fond of cake and To-do lists, and sometimes falls over on her mat. But yoga has taken her on journeys both inside and out, and in this book she travels around Britain to join others in their practice.

Sometimes funny, sometimes touching, Unlikely Positions in Unlikely Places tells of Elizabeth's adventures with her rucksack in 21 British yoga classes, and the characters met along the way. It's a story of ancient wisdom solving modern-day problems, as well as the exultation of finally mastering the Crow.

Also by Robert Wilton

Sherlock & Shakespeare

The greatest detective and the most notorious crimes in all literature: what happens when Sherlock Holmes and Dr John Watson find themselves players in the extraordinary dramas previously told by William Shakespeare? How will they survive, and what new truths will they uncover, amid the wild mysticism of Macbeth's Scotland or the fevered conspiracies of Helsingør?

The Adventure of the Distracted Thane
The Case of the Philosophical Prince

The Gentleman Adventurer

'I've seen chaos in my time: the great bazaar in Constantinople; the retreat after Magersfontein; Frenchmen trying to put up a tent.'

Edwardian entertainment in the company of Harry Delamere as, reluctantly and chaotically, he confronts treachery, conspiracy, murder, revolution, international espionage and persistent interruptions to his perusal of the sporting pages.

Death and the Dreadnought
Poison in Paris
Bolsheviks at the Ballet

The Comptrollerate-General

Immersive historical novels exploring what was really going on in the shadows during the periods of greatest crisis in British history, and showing how one remarkable secret organization has survived centuries of upheaval to maintain stability - for better or for worse. The discovery of a trove of documents under Whitehall, some now published for the first time, has transformed our understanding of the moments when the world turned, and cast new light on the reputation of the Comptrollerate-General for Scrutiny and Survey.

Traitor's Field (1648-51)
Treason's Spring (1792)
Treason's Tide (1805)
The Spider of Sarajevo (1914)

"*A rare clever treat of a novel.*" – The Times

"*Beautifully written, wonderfully clever, this is a triumph.*" – Daily Telegraph

"*A learned, beautifully-written, elegant thriller.*" – The Times

"*Bernard Cornwell meets Ken Follett in a Southwark pub and someone gets coshed. That is to say, great, intelligent fun.*" – Time Out

Also from Elbow Publishing:

Albania and The Balkans: essays in honour of Sir Reginald Hibbert
edited by James Pettifer

A century of Albanian and Balkan history is seen from an unusual variety of perspectives in this collection of essays in honour of a man who parachuted into the country during the Second World War.

Two Summers: Nixon and Trump by Greyhound Bus
by Tim Albert

In 1969 the 22-year-old Tim Albert spent three happy months travelling 12,000 miles around the United States on Greyhound buses. Half a century later to the day he set out to revisit his trip, armed with his original 30,000-word diary.

Mostly We Had It Good: a baby-boomer's journey
by Tim Albert

Teddy Kennedy, EM Forster and Saddam Hussein: an idiosyncratic and insightful look at the second half of the twentieth century, combining recollections, family material and journalism.

About the authors

Elizabeth Gowing and Robert Wilton have lived and worked in the Balkans, and particularly Kosovo, for much of the last twenty years. Their podcast, *A Coffee in the Accursed Mountains*, has explored some of their experiences and interests. They are co-founders, with Ardian Arifaj, of The Ideas Partnership charitable NGO, working to support the education and empowerment of marginalised communities in the region. In 2012 Elizabeth registered a social business, Sa-Punë, offering employment to village and minority community women in Kosovo. In 2016 the President of Kosovo awarded her the Mother Teresa medal for her humanitarian work. In 2017 she was named by British Prime Minister Theresa May a 'point of light' for volunteering around the world. At the end of 2021, Kosovan Prime Minister Albin Kurti appointed her to his cabinet as adviser on community affairs.

Two of her translations of books from Albanian to English have also been published – the biography of Yugoslavia's longest-held political prisoner, Adem Demaçi, and the memoirs of Hasan Prishtina. She is a board member of Faktoje, the Albanian fact-checking NGO.

She runs training for NGOs and others on telling the story of making positive change in the world. She is a frequent contributor to BBC Radio 4 and speaker to groups in the UK. For more of her writing and to join her mailing list, go to www.elizabethgowing.com

Robert was advisor to the Prime Minister of Kosovo in the years leading up to independence, Private Secretary to three UK Secretaries of State for Defence, and head of an international human rights mission in Albania. He is on the boards of diverse NGOs.

A prize-winning historical novelist, he also writes on culture, history and international intervention in the Balkans, and translates Albanian literature into English. He writes for the screen, blogs about film-writing, and teaches film and literature. He's also a practising coach and writing coach. There are curiosities of history and more at www.robertwilton.com.

Printed in Great Britain
by Amazon